AF454156

INTRODUCTION

Data science is often described as the intersection of statistics, computer science, and domain expertise. It is a multidisciplinary field that harnesses the power of data to uncover hidden patterns, make predictions, and inform critical decision-making processes. In an era where data is generated at an unprecedented rate and scale, the role of data scientists has become increasingly critical. They are the detectives of the digital age, using their analytical skills and technical expertise to turn raw data into actionable insights that can drive significant value.

The primary purpose of this book is to demystify the complex world of data science and provide a comprehensive guide for those looking to enter the field or expand their existing knowledge. We will begin by exploring the basics of data science, including key concepts and the fundamental importance of recognizing and understanding data patterns. From there, we will journey through the various stages of a typical data science project, from data collection and cleaning to exploratory analysis and model building.

One of the central themes of this book is the critical importance of pattern recognition within data. Patterns in data can reveal hidden relationships, predict future trends, and provide a competitive edge in various applications. Whether you are a business professional looking to optimize operational efficiencies, a healthcare worker aiming to improve patient outcomes, or a marketer seeking to understand and predict customer behavior, the ability to identify and interpret data patterns is crucial for success.

In addition to exploring technical concepts, we will also address the practical challenges that data scientists face, such as data privacy, integration of disparate data sources, and scalability issues. These challenges require innovative solutions and a steadfast commitment to ethical practices. As we look to the future, we will explore emerging trends and technologies that are shaping the field of data science, from advancements in artificial intelligence to the potential of quantum computing.

This book is not just a technical guide; it is also a narrative that captures the journey of a data scientist. Through personal stories and real-world examples, we will illustrate the diverse paths that lead to a career in data science and the unique experiences that shape each data scientist's perspective.

As you read through these chapters, I encourage you to approach the material with an open and curious mind. Data science is a dynamic and rapidly evolving field, and continuous learning is key to staying relevant and effective. Whether you are a novice just starting out or an experienced practitioner looking to deepen your expertise, I hope this book will provide you with valuable insights and inspire you to explore the vast possibilities that data science has to offer.

CHAPTER 1

INTRODUCTION TO DATA SCIENCE

THE SIGNIFICANCE OF DATA IN THE DIGITAL AGE

In today's digital age, data is often likened to oil, a precious resource driving innovation and informed decision-making across numerous sectors. Data science, a multidisciplinary field that amalgamates statistics, computer science, and specific domain knowledge, has emerged as an indispensable tool for extracting valuable insights from vast quantities of data. This field encompasses the transformation of raw data into actionable insights that can significantly impact various industries, offering a competitive advantage and fostering innovation.

The Data Science Process

The data science process includes several crucial stages, starting with data collection and cleaning to ensure the data's accuracy and reliability. Following this, data undergoes analysis using statistical techniques and machine learning algorithms to identify patterns and trends. Visualization methods subsequently convert these insights into comprehensible formats, making it easier for stakeholders to grasp and utilize the information. This process is iterative, often necessitating revisits to previous steps to refine and enhance the analysis continually, ensuring that the results are accurate and actionable.

Importance of Identifying Data Patterns

Identifying data patterns is a cornerstone of data science, aiding in predicting future trends, optimizing operations, and making informed decisions. Whether in retail, finance, or healthcare, recognizing these patterns is vital for fostering innovation and efficiency. This ability not only enhances decision-making but also provides a competitive edge across various industries. Furthermore, the impact of data science extends beyond business and technology, influencing public policy, environmental conservation, and social sciences, where data-driven insights can yield significant societal benefits, improving the quality of life and informing policy decisions.

The Journey into Data Science

The journey into data science often begins with an insatiable curiosity and a passion for solving complex problems. Aspiring data scientists embark on this path, driven by a desire to understand the underlying mechanisms of data and to leverage it for meaningful outcomes. The field demands a robust foundation in mathematics and statistics, as well as proficiency in programming languages and data manipulation tools, enabling them to handle complex datasets and derive meaningful insights.

The initial stages of learning data science can be overwhelming, characterized by steep learning curves and the need for continuous self-improvement. Aspiring data scientists engage in self-study, enroll in online courses, and participate in extensive experimentation with diverse datasets. This rigorous learning process helps them build resilience and develop problem-solving skills essential for success in the field, preparing them for the challenges they will face in their professional careers.

As data scientists progress in their careers, they encounter various challenges and opportunities for growth. The ability to overcome these challenges, such as dealing with messy, unstructured data and debugging complex algorithms, is crucial for professional development. Each challenge presents an opportunity for learning and discovery, ultimately contributing to a deeper understanding of the data science process, enhancing their ability to extract valuable insights from complex datasets.

The satisfaction of uncovering meaningful insights from raw data, creating predictive models, and realizing real-world applications keeps data scientists motivated. Breakthrough moments, such as developing accurate models or uncovering hidden trends, serve as milestones, marking progress and fueling the desire to learn and achieve more. The journey of a data scientist is a continuous cycle of learning, discovery, and innovation, driven by a passion for making sense of the vast amounts of data available, and the impact they can have on various sectors and society as a whole.

Understanding Data Science

Definition and Scope

Data science is the process of extracting insights from structured and unstructured data using scientific methods, processes, algorithms, and systems. It spans across various domains, including statistics, machine learning, data mining, and big data. This interdisciplinary approach allows data scientists to tackle complex problems and derive meaningful insights from diverse datasets.

Key Components

The main components of data science include data collection, data cleaning, exploratory data analysis (EDA), data modeling, and data visualization. Each of these components plays a crucial role in transforming raw data into actionable insights, ensuring that the analysis is thorough and the results are reliable.

The Evolution of Data Science

Historical Background

The roots of data science can be traced back to statistics and computer science. Over time, advancements in technology and the exponential growth of data have led to the emergence of data science as a distinct field, evolving from simple data analysis to complex machine learning algorithms.

Modern Data Science

Today's data science encompasses a wide range of techniques and tools, from traditional statistical methods to advanced machine learning algorithms and deep learning. The integration of these techniques allows data scientists to tackle complex problems and derive meaningful insights from vast datasets, enabling them to solve real-world challenges effectively.

The Data Science Process

Data Collection

The first step in any data science project involves gathering data from various sources. This can include databases, APIs, web scraping, and even manual data entry. The goal is to compile a comprehensive dataset that captures all relevant information, ensuring that the analysis is based on accurate and complete data.

- **Sources of Data**: Data can come from structured databases, unstructured sources like social media, or semi-structured sources like JSON or XML files. Each source provides different types of data, contributing to a holistic view of the problem at hand.

- **APIs and Web Scraping**: Application Programming Interfaces (APIs) and web scraping techniques are commonly used to extract data from the web, providing access to a wealth of information. These methods allow data scientists to gather large volumes of data efficiently.

- **Manual Data Entry**: In some cases, especially when dealing with niche datasets, manual data entry may be necessary to ensure data completeness. This process, although time-consuming, is crucial for maintaining data integrity.

Data Cleaning

Once data is collected, it must be cleaned to ensure accuracy and consistency. This involves handling missing values, removing duplicates, and correcting errors, making sure that the dataset is ready for analysis.

- **Handling Missing Values**: Techniques such as imputation or removing incomplete records can be employed to address missing data. These methods help maintain the integrity of the dataset, ensuring that the analysis is not biased.

- **Removing Duplicates**: Identifying and removing duplicate records is essential to maintain data integrity. This step ensures that each data point is unique and the analysis is accurate.

- **Correcting Errors**: Ensuring that data is free from errors, such as typos or incorrect values, is crucial for reliable analysis. This step involves verifying and correcting any inconsistencies in the dataset.

Exploratory Data Analysis (EDA)

EDA involves using statistical methods and visualization techniques to understand the data's structure and identify patterns. This step is crucial for gaining insights and guiding further analysis.

- **Statistical Methods**: Descriptive statistics, such as mean, median, and standard deviation, help summarize the data. These methods provide a basic understanding of the dataset, highlighting key characteristics.

- **Visualization Techniques**: Tools like histograms, scatter plots, and box plots are used to visualize data distributions and relationships. These visualizations make it easier to identify patterns and trends in the data.

- **Formulating Hypotheses**: EDA helps formulate hypotheses about the data, guiding further analysis and model development. This step is crucial for identifying potential relationships and trends in the dataset.

Data Modeling

This stage involves building and training models to make predictions or classifications based on the data. The goal is to develop models that can accurately predict or classify new data points.

- **Choosing Algorithms**: Selecting appropriate algorithms, such as linear regression, decision trees, or neural networks, based on the problem and data characteristics. The choice of algorithm depends on the nature of the problem and the type of data available.

- **Training Models**: Using training data to develop models that can accurately predict or classify new data points. This step involves optimizing the model parameters to improve performance.

- **Evaluating Performance**: Assessing model performance using metrics like accuracy, precision, recall, and F1-score to ensure reliability. This step involves testing the model on a validation dataset to ensure it generalizes well to new data.

Data Visualization

The final step is to present the insights in a comprehensible format, using graphs, charts, and dashboards. Effective visualization helps stakeholders understand the analysis results and make informed decisions.

- **Visualization Tools**: Software like Tableau, Power BI, and matplotlib are commonly used to create visual representations of data. These tools allow data scientists to create interactive and informative visualizations.

- **Communicating Insights**: Effective visualization helps stakeholders understand the analysis results and make informed decisions. This step involves presenting the findings in a clear and accessible manner.

- **Iterative Process**: Visualization often leads to new questions and insights, prompting further analysis and refinement of the data. This iterative process ensures that the analysis is thorough and the insights are actionable.

Importance of Pattern Recognition

- **Predicting Trends**: Identifying patterns in data is crucial for predicting future trends, such as sales forecasts or customer behavior. This ability helps businesses plan for the future and make strategic decisions.

- **Optimizing Operations**: Pattern recognition helps optimize operations by identifying inefficiencies and areas for improvement. This step involves analyzing data to find ways to streamline processes and reduce costs.

- **Making Informed Decisions**: Understanding data patterns enables businesses to make informed decisions based on empirical evidence. This step involves using data-driven insights to guide strategic planning and decision-making.

Broad Impact of Data Science

Business and Technology: Data science drives innovation and efficiency in various industries, from retail to healthcare. By leveraging data, businesses can improve their products and services, enhancing customer satisfaction and driving growth.

Public Policy: Data-driven insights can inform public policy decisions, such as resource allocation and social programs. This step involves using data to develop policies that address societal challenges and improve public welfare.

Environmental Conservation: Data science plays a role in environmental conservation efforts, such as monitoring climate change and optimizing resource management. This step involves using data to track environmental trends and develop sustainable solutions.

Social Sciences: Data-driven research in social sciences can uncover trends and patterns that inform policy and societal change. By leveraging data, researchers can gain insights into social behavior, economic trends, and public health issues, contributing to the development of effective interventions and policies that address societal challenges.

The Learning Journey

Curiosity and Passion: The journey begins with a deep curiosity and passion for solving complex problems. Aspiring data scientists are driven by a desire to understand the intricacies of data and its potential to transform industries and society.

Foundational Skills: A strong foundation in mathematics, statistics, and programming is essential. These skills provide the theoretical and technical knowledge necessary for analyzing data and building models.

Continuous Learning: The field of data science is constantly evolving, requiring ongoing learning and adaptation. Data scientists must stay updated with the latest advancements, tools, and best practices to remain effective in their roles.

Hands-On Experience: Practical experience through projects and experimentation is crucial for developing skills. Working with real-world datasets and participating in competitions or hackathons helps build problem-solving abilities and practical knowledge.

Networking and Collaboration: Engaging with the data science community and collaborating with peers enhances learning and growth. Networking provides opportunities for mentorship, knowledge sharing, and career development.

Challenges and Growth

Messy Data: Dealing with messy, unstructured data is a common challenge in data science. Cleaning and preprocessing data to ensure accuracy and consistency is a critical skill.

Complex Algorithms: Debugging and refining complex algorithms requires patience and problem-solving skills. Understanding the underlying principles of algorithms and their applications is crucial for effective modeling.

Scalability: Managing large datasets and ensuring scalability is critical for handling big data. Data scientists must be proficient in using tools and techniques that allow for efficient data processing and analysis.

Ethical Considerations: Ensuring data privacy and ethical use of data is a growing concern in the field. Data scientists must be aware of ethical issues and implement best practices to protect data and maintain trust.

Motivation and Milestones

Breakthrough Moments: Moments of discovery, such as developing accurate models, serve as milestones and keep data scientists motivated. These achievements highlight progress and the impact of their work.

Professional Development: Continuous professional development is essential for staying current with advancements in the field. Data scientists must engage in lifelong learning and skill-building to advance their careers.

Impact and Contribution: The ultimate motivation for many data scientists is the ability to make a positive impact through their work. By uncovering insights and solving problems, they contribute to advancements in various fields and improve outcomes for businesses and society.

By understanding the foundational aspects of data science and appreciating the journey involved, you can embark on your own path with confidence and curiosity. The field of data science offers endless opportunities for discovery and innovation, driven by the ever-growing expanse of data available to us.

CHAPTER 2

THE JOURNEY BEGINS

The journey of a data scientist typically commences with a profound passion for problem-solving and an insatiable curiosity about how things work. This journey often starts with a steep learning curve, characterized by self-study, online courses, and extensive experimentation with various datasets. The path to becoming a data scientist is rarely linear, involving a combination of formal education and hands-on experience. This often includes earning a degree in a related field such as mathematics, statistics, computer science, or engineering, followed by specialized courses and certifications in data science.

The Educational Path

Formal Education: Many data scientists start with a degree in a related field such as mathematics, statistics, computer science, or engineering. These programs provide a solid foundation in the theoretical concepts and technical skills needed in data science.

Specialized Courses: After obtaining a degree, aspiring data scientists often pursue specialized courses and certifications in data science, machine learning, and related fields. These courses offer in-depth knowledge and practical experience.

Online Learning: Platforms like Coursera, edX, and Udacity offer a wide range of online courses in data science. These courses are accessible and flexible, allowing learners to study at their own pace.

The Importance of Hands-On Experience

Experimentation with Datasets: Hands-on experience is crucial for developing practical skills. Aspiring data scientists should experiment with diverse datasets to understand different data types and structures.

Projects and Hackathons: Participating in projects and hackathons provides real-world experience and the opportunity to apply theoretical knowledge. These activities also enhance problem-solving skills and creativity.

Internships and Work Experience: Gaining practical experience through internships or entry-level positions in data science helps bridge the gap between theory and practice. Working on real-world problems and collaborating with experienced professionals is invaluable for gaining practical insights and enhancing one's skillset.

Building a Strong Foundation

Mathematics and Statistics: A solid understanding of mathematics and statistics is essential for data science. Topics such as linear algebra, calculus, probability, and statistical inference are fundamental. These subjects form the backbone of many data science algorithms and methods, enabling data scientists to develop robust and accurate models.

Programming Skills: Proficiency in programming languages like Python and R is crucial. These languages are widely used in data science for data manipulation, analysis, and modeling. Learning these languages provides the technical skills necessary for implementing various data science tasks and solutions.

Data Manipulation Tools: Familiarity with tools like pandas, NumPy, and SQL is important for data cleaning and preprocessing. These tools help manage and manipulate data efficiently, making it easier to prepare datasets for analysis and modeling.

Overcoming Challenges

Dealing with Messy Data: Real-world data is often messy and unstructured. Learning to clean and preprocess data is a critical skill. Techniques for handling missing values, outliers, and inconsistencies are essential for ensuring that the data is suitable for analysis and modeling.

Debugging Complex Algorithms: Debugging code and understanding the intricacies of complex algorithms can be challenging. Persistence and problem-solving skills are key to overcoming these hurdles. Data scientists must develop a deep understanding of how algorithms work and be able to troubleshoot issues that arise during model development and deployment.

Balancing Theory and Practice: Striking a balance between theoretical knowledge and practical application is important. Understanding the theory behind algorithms helps in selecting the right tools and methods for specific problems. At the same time, practical experience provides insights into how these theories are applied in real-world scenarios.

Continuous Learning and Professional Development

Staying Updated: The field of data science is constantly evolving. Staying updated with the latest advancements, tools, and best practices is essential. Subscribing to journals, blogs, and attending conferences helps keep pace with the industry. Continuous learning ensures that data scientists remain relevant and effective in their roles.

Networking and Collaboration: Engaging with the data science community through forums, meetups, and social media platforms provides opportunities for learning, collaboration, and career growth. Networking with peers and mentors is valuable for professional development, offering new perspectives and insights.

Personal Projects: Working on personal projects allows data scientists to explore areas of interest, develop new skills, and build a portfolio. A strong portfolio showcases expertise and creativity to potential employers, demonstrating the ability to apply data science techniques to various problems.

The journey of a data scientist is one of continuous learning, exploration, and growth. By embracing challenges and opportunities, aspiring data scientists can build a successful and fulfilling career in this dynamic field.

CHAPTER 3

TOOLS OF THE TRADE

Navigating the complex landscape of data science requires the right tools and techniques. The journey starts with mastering programming languages such as Python and R. Python, known for its simplicity and extensive libraries like Pandas, NumPy, and Scikit-learn, is a favorite among data scientists. R, renowned for its strong statistical capabilities, is also highly valued, especially in academic and research contexts.

Essential Programming Languages

Python: Python is the most popular language in data science due to its simplicity and versatility. Its extensive libraries, such as Pandas, NumPy, and Scikit-learn, make it ideal for data manipulation, analysis, and machine learning. Python's readability and ease of use make it accessible to beginners, while its powerful libraries and frameworks support complex data science tasks.

R: R is highly regarded for its strong statistical capabilities and is widely used in academic and research settings. It excels in data visualization and statistical analysis, offering a wide range of packages for various statistical techniques and methods.

SQL: SQL (Structured Query Language) is essential for managing and querying databases. It is used to extract, manipulate, and analyze data stored in relational databases. Proficiency in SQL enables data scientists to efficiently work with large datasets and integrate data from multiple sources.

Key Tools and Frameworks

Jupyter Notebooks: Jupyter Notebooks provide an interactive environment for coding, data analysis, and visualization. They are widely used for documenting and sharing data science workflows, allowing for reproducible research and collaboration.

TensorFlow and PyTorch: These are popular frameworks for building and deploying machine learning and deep learning models. TensorFlow is developed by Google, while PyTorch is developed by Facebook. Both frameworks offer extensive tools and libraries for developing sophisticated models and applications.

Hadoop and Spark: These tools are vital for handling big data. Hadoop is a distributed storage and processing framework, while Spark is a fast and general-purpose cluster-computing system. Both tools are essential for processing large-scale datasets and performing advanced analytics.

Tableau and Power BI: These data visualization tools enable the creation of interactive dashboards and visualizations. They help in communicating insights effectively to stakeholders, making complex data more accessible and understandable.

Data Manipulation and Analysis

Pandas: Pandas is a powerful Python library for data manipulation and analysis. It provides data structures like DataFrames, which are essential for handling structured data. Pandas simplifies data cleaning, transformation, and analysis, making it a crucial tool for data scientists.

NumPy: NumPy is a fundamental package for numerical computing in Python. It provides support for arrays, matrices, and a wide range of mathematical functions. NumPy is used for performing efficient numerical operations, supporting various scientific and engineering applications.

Scikit-learn: Scikit-learn is a comprehensive library for machine learning in Python. It offers simple and efficient tools for data mining and data analysis, including algorithms for classification, regression, clustering, and dimensionality reduction.

Data Visualization

Matplotlib and Seaborn: These Python libraries are used for creating static, animated, and interactive visualizations. Matplotlib is highly customizable, while Seaborn is built on top of Matplotlib and provides a high-level interface for drawing attractive statistical graphics. Both libraries are essential for creating detailed and informative visualizations.

Plotly: Plotly is a graphing library that makes interactive, publication-quality graphs online. It is used for creating complex visualizations, including 3D plots and maps. Plotly's interactive features make it ideal for presenting data insights in an engaging and accessible way.

Big Data Technologies

Hadoop: Hadoop is an open-source framework that allows for the distributed storage and processing of large datasets across clusters of computers. It is used for big data analytics and supports various components, including HDFS (Hadoop Distributed File System) and MapReduce. Hadoop's scalability and fault-tolerance make it suitable for handling massive amounts of data.

Spark: Apache Spark is a unified analytics engine for large-scale data processing. It provides high-level APIs in Java, Scala, Python, and R, and an optimized engine that supports general execution graphs. Spark's in-memory processing capabilities make it significantly faster than traditional disk-based processing frameworks.

Data Management and Storage

SQL Databases: SQL databases, such as MySQL, PostgreSQL, and Microsoft SQL Server, are essential for storing and managing structured data. They provide robust querying capabilities and are widely used in data warehousing and business intelligence applications.

NoSQL Databases: NoSQL databases, such as MongoDB, Cassandra, and Redis, are designed for unstructured or semi-structured data. They offer flexibility in data modeling and are suitable for handling large volumes of diverse data types.

Data Lakes: Data lakes, such as Amazon S3 and Azure Data Lake, provide scalable storage for vast amounts of raw data. They support various data formats and enable efficient data ingestion, storage, and processing.

Cloud Platforms: Cloud platforms, such as AWS, Google Cloud, and Microsoft Azure, offer comprehensive data storage and processing services. They provide scalability, flexibility, and advanced tools for data management, machine learning, and analytics.

Data Visualization Tools

Tableau: Tableau is a powerful data visualization tool that enables the creation of interactive and shareable dashboards. It allows users to connect to various data sources, perform data analysis, and visualize insights through intuitive drag-and-drop interfaces.

Power BI: Power BI, developed by Microsoft, is another popular data visualization tool. It integrates with various data sources, supports real-time data analysis, and provides robust reporting and dashboarding capabilities.

Matplotlib and Seaborn: These Python libraries are widely used for creating static, animated, and interactive visualizations. Matplotlib provides a flexible foundation for custom plots, while Seaborn builds on Matplotlib to offer more aesthetically pleasing and informative statistical graphics.

Plotly: Plotly is a graphing library that supports interactive and publication-quality visualizations. It is particularly useful for creating complex visualizations, such as 3D plots, heatmaps, and interactive dashboards.

Collaborative Tools

Git and GitHub: Version control systems like Git and platforms like GitHub are essential for collaboration and code management. They allow data scientists to track changes, collaborate with team members, and maintain version control for their projects. These tools are crucial for managing code repositories, facilitating collaboration on large projects, and ensuring that all team members have access to the latest code versions.

Jupyter Notebooks: Jupyter Notebooks provide an interactive environment for coding, data analysis, and visualization. They are widely used for documenting data science workflows, sharing analyses, and creating reproducible research. The ability to combine code, visualizations, and narrative text makes Jupyter Notebooks a versatile tool for collaborative data science projects.

Advanced Analytical Tools

Apache Spark: Apache Spark is a unified analytics engine for large-scale data processing. It supports in-memory processing, making it significantly faster than traditional disk-based processing frameworks like Hadoop. Spark provides high-level APIs in Java, Scala, Python, and R, and is used for big data analytics, machine learning, and stream processing. Its ability to handle large datasets and perform complex computations makes it a valuable tool for data scientists.

Hadoop: Hadoop is an open-source framework that allows for the distributed storage and processing of large datasets across clusters of computers. It is used for big data analytics and supports various components, including HDFS (Hadoop Distributed File System) and MapReduce. Hadoop's scalability and reliability make it suitable for managing and analyzing large volumes of data.

Natural Language Processing (NLP) Tools

NLTK: The Natural Language Toolkit (NLTK) is a comprehensive library for natural language processing in Python. It provides tools for text processing, tokenization, stemming, and more. NLTK is widely used for building applications that process and analyze human language data.

spaCy: spaCy is an open-source library for advanced NLP in Python. It is designed for large-scale information extraction and natural language understanding, providing efficient and fast NLP processing. SpaCy is known for its performance and ease of use, making it a popular choice for NLP tasks.

Gensim: Gensim is a library for topic modeling and document similarity analysis. It is widely used for tasks such as building word embeddings and performing semantic analysis. Gensim's efficient algorithms make it suitable for processing large text corpora.

Key Points to Remember

- **Importance of Tools**: The right tools are essential for efficient and effective data science work. They enable data scientists to manage, analyze, and visualize data, and to build and deploy machine learning models. Mastery of these tools is crucial for success in the field.

- **Continuous Learning**: The field of data science is dynamic, with new tools and technologies emerging regularly. Continuous learning and adaptation are crucial for staying current and effective. Data scientists must be committed to lifelong learning to keep up with industry advancements.

- **Collaboration**: Collaboration tools like Git and Jupyter Notebooks are vital for working effectively with team members and sharing findings. Effective collaboration enhances productivity and innovation in data science projects.

- **Visualization**: Data visualization tools are crucial for communicating insights and making data-driven decisions. Visualizations make complex data more accessible and understandable, facilitating informed decision-making. By mastering these tools and continuously updating their skillset, data scientists can tackle a wide range of challenges and deliver impactful results in their work. The ability to adapt to new technologies and methodologies is essential for remaining effective and relevant in the ever-evolving field of data science.

CHAPTER 4

DIVING INTO THE DATA

At the core of every data science initiative is the data itself. The journey starts with data collection, which involves gathering information from various sources such as databases, APIs, and web scraping. This data is frequently messy, incomplete, and unstructured, necessitating substantial effort to clean and preprocess it. Data collection is a critical phase that lays the groundwork for the entire project. It involves defining the data requirements, identifying relevant data sources, and establishing methods for data acquisition. Sometimes, data scientists might need to generate synthetic data or employ data augmentation techniques to enhance the dataset's quality and comprehensiveness.

Data Collection

Sources of Data: Data can come from various sources, including structured databases, unstructured sources like social media, and semi-structured sources like JSON or XML files. Identifying the right sources is crucial for obtaining relevant and comprehensive data that accurately represents the problem space.

APIs and Web Scraping: Application Programming Interfaces (APIs) and web scraping techniques are commonly used to extract data from the web. APIs provide programmatic access to data, allowing for automated data retrieval, while web scraping involves extracting data from web pages through automated scripts.

Manual Data Entry: In some cases, especially when dealing with niche datasets, manual data entry may be necessary to ensure data completeness. This process involves manually inputting data into a system, which can be time-consuming but is sometimes essential for capturing specific or detailed information that automated methods might miss.

Data Cleaning

Once data is collected, it must be cleaned to ensure accuracy and consistency. This involves handling missing values, removing duplicates, and correcting errors to create a reliable dataset.

Handling Missing Values: Techniques such as imputation (filling in missing values with estimated values) or removing incomplete records can be employed to address missing data. The choice of technique depends on the nature and extent of the missing data and the impact on the analysis.

Removing Duplicates: Identifying and removing duplicate records is essential to maintain data integrity. Duplicates can arise from multiple data sources or repeated entries, leading to inflated or misleading results if not addressed.

Correcting Errors: Ensuring that data is free from errors, such as typos or incorrect values, is crucial for reliable analysis. This may involve validating data against known standards, cross-referencing with other sources, or using automated error detection algorithms.

Exploratory Data Analysis (EDA)

Exploratory Data Analysis (EDA) involves using statistical methods and visualization techniques to understand the data's structure and identify patterns. It is a critical step in the data science process, as it helps formulate hypotheses and guides further analysis.

Statistical Methods: Descriptive statistics, such as mean, median, standard deviation, and percentiles, help summarize the data and provide insights into its distribution and central tendency. These measures offer a quick overview of the dataset's key characteristics.

Visualization Techniques: Tools like histograms, scatter plots, box plots, and heatmaps are used to visualize data distributions, relationships, and correlations. Visualization helps identify outliers, trends, and patterns that are not immediately apparent from raw data, making complex datasets more accessible.

Formulating Hypotheses: EDA helps formulate hypotheses about the data, guiding the selection of features and models for further analysis. It involves exploring different aspects of the data to uncover underlying structures and relationships, which can inform the development of predictive models and analytical strategies.

Data Transformation

Data transformation involves converting raw data into a format suitable for analysis. This may include normalizing data, creating new features, and encoding categorical variables to improve the dataset's quality and the accuracy of subsequent analyses.

Normalization: Normalizing data involves scaling numerical features to a standard range, typically 0 to 1. This ensures that all features contribute equally to the analysis, preventing any single feature from disproportionately influencing the results due to its scale.

Feature Engineering: Feature engineering involves creating new features from existing data to improve model performance. This may include combining features, extracting components, or creating interaction terms that capture more complex relationships within the data.

Encoding Categorical Variables: Categorical variables need to be converted into numerical format for analysis. Techniques such as one-hot encoding and label encoding are commonly used, transforming categorical data into a form that machine learning algorithms can process effectively.

Data Modeling

This stage involves building and training models to make predictions or classifications based on the data. It is a critical phase that transforms insights into actionable outcomes, enabling the practical application of data science findings.

Choosing Algorithms: Selecting appropriate algorithms is based on the problem and data characteristics. Common algorithms include linear regression, logistic regression, decision trees, random forests, and neural networks. The choice of algorithm depends on factors such as the nature of the target variable, the size and complexity of the dataset, and the specific goals of the analysis.

Training Models: Using training data to develop models that can accurately predict or classify new data points. This involves splitting the data into training and testing sets, training the model on the training set, and validating it on the testing set to ensure its generalizability.

Evaluating Performance: Assessing model performance using metrics like accuracy, precision, recall, F1-score, and the area under the ROC curve (AUC-ROC). These metrics help determine the model's effectiveness and guide further tuning and improvement, ensuring that the model meets the desired performance criteria.

Data Visualization

The final step is to present the insights in a comprehensible format, using graphs, charts, and dashboards. Effective visualization helps communicate the results to stakeholders and supports decision-making by making complex data more accessible and understandable.

Visualization Tools: Software like Tableau, Power BI, and matplotlib are commonly used to create visual representations of data. These tools offer a range of features to create interactive, dynamic, and static visualizations that can help convey complex data insights in an understandable and impactful way. They support a variety of visualization types, including bar charts, line graphs, pie charts, scatter plots, heatmaps, and dashboards. These visualizations enable data scientists to present their findings in a manner that is easily interpretable by stakeholders, facilitating data-driven decision-making.

Communicating Insights: Effective data visualization is about more than just creating charts and graphs; it is about telling a story with data. By carefully selecting the right types of visualizations and combining them to highlight key insights, data scientists can make their analyses more compelling and persuasive. Good visualizations should be clear, concise, and focused on the most important aspects of the data, guiding the viewer through the narrative of the findings.

Iterative Process: Visualization often leads to new questions and insights, prompting further analysis and refinement of the data. As stakeholders review visualizations, they may identify additional areas for investigation or require further breakdowns of the data. This iterative process helps ensure that the analysis is comprehensive and that all relevant insights are uncovered.

Practical Examples and Case Studies

Retail Industry: In the retail industry, data scientists use customer transaction data to understand purchasing behavior, segment customers, and optimize inventory. For example, by analyzing sales data, a retailer might identify which products are frequently bought together, leading to strategic placement in stores or targeted marketing campaigns. Additionally, predictive models can forecast demand, helping retailers manage stock levels and reduce waste. By understanding seasonal trends and customer preferences, retailers can make data-driven decisions that enhance customer satisfaction and boost sales.

Healthcare Sector: In healthcare, data scientists analyze patient records to identify patterns related to disease outbreaks, treatment efficacy, and patient outcomes. For example, analyzing electronic health records (EHRs) can help predict which patients are at higher risk for certain conditions, enabling proactive interventions. Data visualization can show the spread of diseases across different regions, aiding in resource allocation and public health responses. By integrating various health data sources, healthcare providers can improve patient care, reduce costs, and develop more effective treatment plans.

Financial Services: In financial services, data scientists work on detecting fraudulent transactions, assessing credit risk, and optimizing investment strategies. For instance, by analyzing transaction data, banks can build models to flag potentially fraudulent activities in real-time, protecting customers and reducing financial losses. Visualization tools can help present these findings to fraud analysts, enhancing their ability to make informed decisions quickly. Additionally, predictive analytics can help financial institutions identify high-risk borrowers and tailor credit offers to minimize default rates, improving overall financial stability.

Challenges and Solutions in Data Handling

Scalability Issues: As the volume of data grows, scalability becomes a significant challenge. Handling large datasets efficiently requires robust data storage solutions and processing power. Tools like Hadoop and Spark are designed to handle big data, providing the infrastructure necessary to store and process massive datasets across distributed systems. Implementing cloud-based solutions can also offer scalable resources that adapt to changing data needs.

Data Privacy and Security: Ensuring data privacy and security is paramount, especially when handling sensitive information such as personal health records or financial data. Data scientists must implement robust security measures to protect data from breaches and unauthorized access. Techniques like data anonymization, encryption, and secure access protocols are critical for maintaining data integrity and confidentiality. Adhering to data protection regulations, such as GDPR and HIPAA, ensures compliance and builds trust with data subjects.

Integrating Disparate Data Sources: Integrating data from multiple sources, each with different formats and structures, can be challenging. Data integration tools and ETL (Extract, Transform, Load) processes are essential for harmonizing data and ensuring consistency. These tools help clean, transform, and load data into a unified system, making it ready for analysis. Developing standardized data schemas and employing middleware solutions can facilitate seamless data integration and improve overall data quality.

Ethical Considerations in Data Handling

Bias in Data: One of the ethical challenges in data science is addressing bias in data. Bias can arise from various sources, including sampling methods, data collection processes, and inherent biases in the data itself. Data scientists must be vigilant in identifying and mitigating bias to ensure fair and unbiased analysis. This involves using techniques like re-sampling, adjusting weights, and employing fairness-aware algorithms. Regular audits and validation checks are also necessary to detect and correct biases that might influence the results, ensuring that the outcomes are equitable and representative.

Transparency and Accountability: Ensuring transparency and accountability in data analysis is crucial for building trust with stakeholders. Data scientists should document their methods, assumptions, and decision-making processes clearly. This transparency allows others to understand, replicate, and validate the analysis, promoting accountability and integrity in data science practices. Providing clear explanations of the models and their limitations helps stakeholders make informed decisions based on a thorough understanding of the analysis.

Continuous Learning and Adaptation

Staying Updated with Tools and Technologies: The field of data science is rapidly evolving, with new tools, technologies, and methodologies emerging regularly. Continuous learning and professional development are essential for data scientists to stay current and effective in their work. This includes participating in workshops, taking online courses, attending conferences, and engaging with the data science community. Keeping up with the latest research papers and industry trends is also crucial for staying at the forefront of the field.

Adapting to New Challenges: Data scientists must be adaptable and ready to tackle new challenges as they arise. Whether it's dealing with new types of data, addressing emerging ethical concerns, or leveraging the latest advancements in machine learning, the ability to adapt and innovate is critical for success in the field. Flexibility and a proactive approach to problem-solving enable data scientists to navigate the complexities of their work and continue delivering valuable insights.

Key Points to Remember

Foundational Steps: The data science process begins with data collection, cleaning, and exploratory data analysis. These foundational steps are crucial for ensuring the quality and reliability of the data. Without a solid foundation, subsequent analyses and model-building efforts are likely to be flawed or less effective.

Visualization: Data visualization is a powerful tool for communicating insights. Effective visualizations help stakeholders understand and act on the findings, making data-driven decision-making possible. Visualizations should be clear, intuitive, and designed to highlight the most critical aspects of the data.

Real-World Applications: Data science has practical applications across various industries, from retail and healthcare to finance and beyond. These applications demonstrate the value of data-driven insights in solving real-world problems, improving efficiency, and driving innovation.

Ethical Practices: Ethical considerations, such as addressing bias and ensuring transparency, are essential for responsible data science. Upholding ethical standards builds trust and integrity in the analysis, ensuring that the results are fair, unbiased, and trustworthy.

Continuous Learning: The field of data science is dynamic and ever-changing. Continuous learning and adaptation are vital for staying relevant and effective in the profession. Embracing new tools, methodologies, and best practices is essential for maintaining a competitive edge and continuing to deliver impactful results.

By diving into the data and mastering these steps, data scientists can unlock valuable insights and drive meaningful impact in their work. The journey is challenging but rewarding, filled with opportunities for discovery and innovation. Mastery of data science tools, techniques, and ethical practices ensures that data scientists are well-equipped to tackle complex problems and deliver solutions that benefit businesses, industries, and society as a whole.

CHAPTER 5

IDENTIFYING PATTERNS

The ability to identify patterns in data is what distinguishes data scientists. Pattern recognition involves using algorithms to detect regularities and structures within data. Techniques like clustering, classification, and association rule learning are commonly used to uncover patterns that provide valuable insights. Pattern recognition is fundamental to data science, enabling the discovery of meaningful relationships and trends that drive decision-making and innovation.

For example, clustering algorithms group similar data points together, helping identify natural segments within the data. This can be useful in customer segmentation, where businesses tailor their marketing strategies to different customer groups. Clustering techniques such as K-means, hierarchical clustering, and DBSCAN are widely used to explore the inherent structure of the data and uncover hidden patterns. Classification algorithms, on the other hand, assign data points to predefined categories, which is essential in applications like email spam detection and disease diagnosis. Popular classification algorithms include decision trees, support vector machines, and neural networks, each with its strengths and use cases.

Clustering Techniques

- K-means Clustering: K-means is one of the most popular clustering algorithms. It partitions the data into K clusters, where each data point belongs to the cluster with the nearest mean. The algorithm iteratively updates the cluster centroids until convergence. K-means is widely used for customer segmentation, image compression, and anomaly detection, as it effectively identifies natural groupings within a dataset by minimizing the within-cluster variance.

- Hierarchical Clustering: Hierarchical clustering builds a hierarchy of clusters using either an agglomerative (bottom-up) or divisive (top-down) approach. In agglomerative clustering, each data point starts as its own cluster, and pairs of clusters are merged iteratively based on their similarity. In divisive clustering, the entire dataset starts as one cluster, and it is recursively split into smaller clusters. This technique is useful for creating dendrograms that illustrate the hierarchical relationships between clusters, providing a visual and intuitive representation of the data's structure.

- DBSCAN (Density-Based Spatial Clustering of Applications with Noise: DBSCAN is a density-based clustering algorithm that groups data points based on their density. It can identify clusters of arbitrary shape and is robust to noise and outliers. DBSCAN is particularly effective for spatial data and applications such as geographical mapping and image analysis, as it does not require specifying the number of clusters in advance and can automatically discover the optimal number of clusters based on the density of the data points.

Classification Techniques

- Decision Trees: Decision trees are a popular classification method that models decisions and their possible consequences in a tree-like structure. Each node represents a decision point, and branches represent the possible outcomes. Decision trees are easy to interpret and visualize, making them suitable for a wide range of applications, including medical diagnosis and customer churn prediction. They work by recursively splitting the data into subsets based on the most significant attribute at each node, creating a straightforward path from the root to the leaves.

- Support Vector Machines (SVM: SVM is a powerful classification algorithm that finds the optimal hyperplane separating different classes in the feature space. It is effective for high-dimensional data and is used in applications such as text classification and image recognition. SVM aims to maximize the margin between the closest points of the classes, known as support vectors, ensuring a robust separation even in complex and high-dimensional spaces.

- Neural Networks: Neural networks are a class of machine learning models inspired by the structure and function of the human brain. They consist of interconnected layers of nodes (neurons) that process and learn from data. Neural networks are highly flexible and can model complex, non-linear relationships. They are widely used in applications such as speech recognition, image classification, and natural language processing. Neural networks can capture intricate patterns through multiple layers of transformations, making them particularly suited for deep learning tasks involving vast and complex datasets.

Association Rule Learning

- Apriori Algorithm: The Apriori algorithm is used for mining frequent itemsets and discovering association rules in transactional datasets. It identifies itemsets that frequently occur together and generates rules that describe the relationships between these itemsets. Apriori is commonly used in market basket analysis to identify products that are often purchased together. By iteratively exploring combinations of items and applying a threshold for minimum support, Apriori efficiently discovers significant associations in large datasets.

- FP-Growth Algorithm: FP-Growth (Frequent Pattern Growth) is an efficient algorithm for mining frequent itemsets without candidate generation. It constructs a compact representation of the dataset called an FP-tree and uses it to mine frequent patterns directly. FP-Growth is faster and more scalable than Apriori for large datasets. By compressing the dataset into an FP-tree, FP-Growth reduces the complexity of the frequent pattern mining process, allowing for rapid and scalable analysis.

Challenges in Pattern Recognition

- High Dimensionality: One of the significant challenges in pattern recognition is dealing with high-dimensional data, where the number of features is large. High dimensionality can lead to overfitting and make the models computationally expensive. Dimensionality reduction techniques, such as Principal Component Analysis (PCA) and t-Distributed Stochastic Neighbor Embedding (t-SNE), are used to address this challenge. By reducing the number of features while preserving the essential information, these techniques help simplify the data and enhance the efficiency and accuracy of pattern recognition models.

- Noise and Outliers: Noise and outliers can obscure meaningful patterns in the data. Identifying and handling these anomalies is crucial for accurate pattern recognition. Techniques such as robust statistics, anomaly detection, and outlier removal are employed to mitigate the impact of noise and outliers. By filtering out irrelevant or erroneous data points, these methods improve the quality and reliability of the analysis, ensuring that the identified patterns are truly representative of the underlying data.

- Imbalanced Data: Imbalanced datasets, where some classes are underrepresented, can bias the pattern recognition models. Techniques such as resampling, synthetic data generation (e.g., SMOTE), and cost-sensitive learning are used to address class imbalance and improve model performance. By ensuring that all classes are adequately represented in the training data, these techniques help create more balanced and robust models that perform well across different classes, leading to more accurate and fair pattern recognition.

Ethical Considerations in Pattern Recognition

- Bias and Fairness: Bias in data and models can lead to unfair outcomes and discrimination. Ensuring fairness and mitigating bias is essential for ethical pattern recognition. Techniques such as fairness-aware algorithms, bias detection, and re-sampling methods are employed to address these issues. By actively identifying and correcting biases, data scientists can develop models that provide equitable and unbiased insights, fostering trust and fairness in data-driven decision-making processes.

- Transparency and Interpretability: Transparent and interpretable models are crucial for building trust with stakeholders. Techniques such as model explainability tools (e.g., SHAP, LIME) and rule-based models are used to enhance transparency and interpretability. By providing clear explanations of how models make decisions, these tools help stakeholders understand and trust the results, facilitating informed decision-making and ethical use of pattern recognition technologies.

Future Directions in Pattern Recognition

- Deep Learning: Deep learning techniques, such as convolutional neural networks (CNNs) and recurrent neural networks (RNNs), are increasingly being used for complex pattern recognition tasks. Deep learning techniques, such as convolutional neural networks (CNNs) and recurrent neural networks (RNNs), are increasingly being used for complex pattern recognition tasks. These models can automatically learn hierarchical features from data, making them suitable for applications like image and speech recognition. CNNs, in particular, excel at processing structured grid data such as images, by capturing spatial hierarchies through convolutional layers. RNNs are well-suited for sequential data, such as time series and natural language, due to their ability to maintain information across time steps.

- Transfer Learning: Transfer learning, where models pre-trained on large datasets are fine-tuned for specific tasks, is becoming popular in pattern recognition. It allows leveraging existing knowledge to improve performance on new tasks with limited data. For instance, a neural network trained on a large image dataset can be fine-tuned for a specific medical imaging task, significantly enhancing the accuracy and efficiency of the model without the need for extensive training data.

- Explainable AI (XAI): Explainable AI is an emerging field focused on making machine learning models more transparent and interpretable. XAI techniques help stakeholders understand how models make decisions, increasing trust and facilitating ethical use of pattern recognition. Methods such as SHAP (SHapley Additive exPlanations) and LIME (Local Interpretable Model-agnostic Explanations) provide insights into which features most influence a model's predictions, making it easier to interpret complex models.

Key Points to Remember

Importance of Pattern Recognition: Identifying patterns in data is crucial for deriving meaningful insights and making informed decisions. It enables predictive analytics, optimization, and innovation across various industries. Understanding these patterns allows organizations to leverage data effectively to drive strategic initiatives and operational improvements.

Techniques and Algorithms: Various techniques, such as clustering, classification, and association rule learning, are used for pattern recognition. Choosing the right algorithm depends on the specific problem and data characteristics. Familiarity with a range of algorithms and their appropriate applications enhances a data scientist's ability to tackle diverse challenges effectively.

Real-World Applications: Pattern recognition has practical applications in industries such as retail, healthcare, finance, manufacturing, and energy. These applications demonstrate the value of data-driven insights in solving real-world problems. By applying pattern recognition techniques, organizations can enhance efficiency, improve decision-making, and gain a competitive edge.

Challenges and Solutions: High dimensionality, noise, and imbalanced data are common challenges in pattern recognition. Techniques such as dimensionality reduction, anomaly detection, and resampling are used to address these challenges. Developing robust solutions to these issues ensures that the patterns identified are accurate, reliable, and actionable.

Ethical Considerations: Ensuring fairness, transparency, and interpretability is essential for ethical pattern recognition. Bias detection, fairness-aware algorithms, and explainable AI techniques are crucial for responsible use. Adhering to ethical guidelines helps build trust and ensures that data-driven insights are used to benefit all stakeholders equitably.

Future Directions: Advances in deep learning, transfer learning, and explainable AI are shaping the future of pattern recognition. These innovations hold promise for more accurate, efficient, and ethical pattern recognition. Staying abreast of these developments enables data scientists to leverage cutting-edge techniques and tools to enhance their analyses and applications.

By mastering pattern recognition techniques and understanding their applications, data scientists can unlock valuable insights and drive meaningful impact in their work. The ability to identify and interpret patterns in data is a powerful tool for solving complex problems and achieving strategic goals. Pattern recognition not only enhances decision-making and operational efficiency but also drives innovation and growth across various domains.

CHAPTER 6

NAVIGATING THROUGH NOISE

In the world of data, not all information is useful. Noise refers to irrelevant or random data that can obscure meaningful patterns. Differentiating signal (useful information) from noise is a critical skill for data scientists. The ability to filter out noise and focus on the signal is essential for deriving accurate and reliable insights from data.

Techniques for Enhancing Signal-to-Noise Ratio

Feature Selection: Feature selection involves identifying the most relevant variables for analysis, reducing the model's complexity and improving its performance. Methods such as recursive feature elimination (RFE) and LASSO regression are commonly used for feature selection, helping isolate the most predictive variables. By focusing on the most important features, data scientists can improve model interpretability and reduce the risk of overfitting.

Dimensionality Reduction: Dimensionality reduction techniques like Principal Component Analysis (PCA) and t-Distributed Stochastic Neighbor Embedding (t-SNE) simplify the data by reducing the number of variables while retaining essential information. PCA and other techniques like t-SNE and UMAP enable data scientists to visualize high-dimensional data and uncover underlying patterns. These techniques help manage the complexity of large datasets, making it easier to identify the signal amidst the noise.

Filtering: Filtering techniques involve removing noise from the data, enhancing the signal. This can include smoothing methods, such as moving averages, and frequency-based filtering techniques like Fourier transforms. By applying these techniques, data scientists can reduce the impact of random fluctuations and focus on the true underlying patterns.

Practical Examples

Financial Data Analysis: In financial data analysis, noise can arise from market volatility, irregular trading patterns, and outlier events. Techniques such as moving averages and Bollinger Bands are used to smooth time series data, highlighting underlying trends and reducing the impact of short-term fluctuations. These methods help financial analysts identify significant trends and make informed investment decisions.

Sensor Data Processing: In industrial applications, sensor data is often noisy due to environmental factors and hardware limitations. Filtering techniques, such as Kalman filters and low-pass filters, are used to remove noise from sensor readings, ensuring accurate monitoring and control of processes. By enhancing the signal quality, these techniques improve the reliability and effectiveness of industrial systems.

Image Processing: In image processing, noise can distort visual information, making it challenging to identify patterns. Techniques like Gaussian filtering and median filtering are used to reduce noise in images, enhancing the quality and accuracy of image analysis. These methods are essential for applications such as medical imaging, where clear and precise visual information is crucial for accurate diagnosis.

Best Practices for Effective Data Analysis

Cross-Validation: Cross-validation techniques, such as k-fold cross-validation, ensure that models generalize well to new data. By partitioning the data into training and validation sets multiple times, cross-validation provides a robust assessment of model performance and reduces the risk of overfitting. This practice helps data scientists evaluate the true predictive power of their models.

Regularization: Regularization methods like ridge and lasso regression prevent overfitting by penalizing large coefficients in the model. These techniques help balance model complexity and performance, ensuring that the model captures the underlying patterns without fitting to noise. Regularization is particularly useful when dealing with high-dimensional data, where the risk of overfitting is high.

Anomaly Detection: Anomaly detection techniques, such as isolation forests and clustering-based methods, help identify and address outliers and noise in the data. By detecting anomalies, data scientists can remove or adjust these points, improving the overall quality of the analysis. Anomaly detection is crucial for maintaining data integrity and ensuring that the models are trained on representative data.

Challenges in Differentiating Signal from Noise

High Dimensionality High-dimensional data can make it challenging to distinguish between signal and noise. Dimensionality reduction techniques and feature selection are essential for managing complexity and enhancing signal detection. By reducing the number of variables, data scientists can focus on the most relevant features and improve the accuracy of their analyses.

Dynamic and Non-Stationary Data: In many applications, data is dynamic and non-stationary, meaning that the underlying patterns change over time. Adaptive filtering techniques and time series analysis methods are used to account for these changes and maintain accurate signal detection. These techniques help data scientists adapt to evolving patterns and ensure that their models remain effective over time.

Complex Interactions: In complex systems, interactions between variables can create intricate patterns that are difficult to separate from noise. Advanced machine learning algorithms, such as ensemble methods and deep learning, are used to model these interactions and enhance signal detection. By capturing the complex relationships between variables, these methods improve the ability to identify meaningful patterns.

Key Points to Remember

Importance of Signal-to-Noise Ratio: Enhancing the signal-to-noise ratio is crucial for accurate and reliable data analysis. Techniques like feature selection, dimensionality reduction, and filtering are essential for isolating meaningful patterns from irrelevant data. Improving the signal-to-noise ratio helps in deriving clear and actionable insights, which are fundamental for data-driven decision-making.

Practical Applications: Noise reduction techniques are applied in various fields, including finance, manufacturing, and image processing, to improve the quality and reliability of data-driven insights. These applications highlight the versatility and importance of noise reduction in enhancing the effectiveness of data analysis across different industries.

Challenges and Solutions: High dimensionality, dynamic data, and complex interactions pose challenges in differentiating signal from noise. Advanced techniques and best practices, such as cross-validation and regularization, help address these challenges.

Implementing these solutions ensures that the identified patterns are robust and representative of the underlying data.

By mastering the techniques and principles of noise reduction, data scientists can ensure that their analyses are accurate, reliable, and impactful. Navigating through noise is a fundamental skill that enables data scientists to extract meaningful insights and drive informed decision-making. Effective noise reduction not only enhances the quality of data analysis but also contributes to the development of robust and trustworthy models, ultimately supporting better outcomes in various applications.

CHAPTER 7

MACHINE LEARNING MODELS

Machine learning is a pivotal aspect of contemporary data science. It involves teaching algorithms to learn from data and make predictions or decisions without explicit programming. Machine learning models fall into three primary categories: supervised, unsupervised, and reinforcement learning. Each category includes various algorithms and techniques suited for different problems and data types, enabling data scientists to address a broad spectrum of analytical challenges.

Supervised Learning

Supervised learning entails training models on labeled data, enabling the algorithm to predict the output based on input features. Common algorithms in this category include linear regression, logistic regression, decision trees, random forests, support vector machines, and neural networks. These models are extensively used for tasks such as classification, regression, and time-series forecasting, helping solve problems ranging from predicting housing prices to diagnosing diseases.

Linear Regression: Linear regression is used to predict a continuous target variable based on one or more input features. It assumes a linear relationship between the input features and the target variable. Linear regression is simple and interpretable, making it suitable for many applications, such as predicting house prices or sales. The model minimizes the sum of the squared differences between the observed and predicted values, ensuring the best fit line.

Logistic Regression: Logistic regression is used for binary classification problems, where the goal is to predict one of two possible outcomes. It models the probability of the target variable using a logistic function. Logistic regression is widely used in applications such as spam detection and disease diagnosis. The logistic function ensures the output is between 0 and 1, making it ideal for probability estimation.

Decision Trees: Decision trees are tree-like models that make decisions based on a series of rules derived from the input features. They are intuitive and easy to visualize, making them suitable for applications where interpretability is important, such as credit scoring and customer segmentation. Decision trees split the data into branches based on feature values, creating a path from root to leaf that represents the decision rules.

Random Forests: Random forests are an ensemble method that combines multiple decision trees to improve accuracy and robustness. Each tree in the forest is trained on a random subset of the data, and the final prediction is made by averaging the predictions of all trees. Random forests are used in a wide range of applications, including image classification and fraud detection. The ensemble approach helps reduce overfitting and increases model stability.

Support Vector Machines (SVM): SVM is a powerful classification algorithm that finds the optimal hyperplane separating different classes in the feature space. It is effective for high-dimensional data and is used in applications such as text classification and image recognition. SVM aims to maximize the margin between the closest points of different classes, ensuring a clear separation.

Neural Networks: Neural networks are a class of machine learning models inspired by the structure and function of the human brain. They consist of interconnected layers of nodes (neurons) that process and learn from data. Neural networks are highly flexible and can model complex, non-linear relationships. They are widely used in applications such as speech recognition, image classification, and natural language processing. Neural networks can capture intricate patterns through multiple layers of transformations, making them particularly suited for deep learning tasks involving vast and complex datasets.

Unsupervised Learning

In contrast, unsupervised learning deals with unlabeled data, where the algorithm identifies patterns and structures without predefined labels. Typical unsupervised learning tasks include clustering, association, and dimensionality reduction. Algorithms like K-means clustering, hierarchical clustering, and DBSCAN group similar data points together, while techniques such as principal component analysis (PCA) and t-distributed stochastic neighbor embedding (t-SNE) reduce data dimensionality and visualize complex relationships. Unsupervised learning is essential for exploratory data analysis and finding hidden structures within the data.

K-means Clustering: K-means is one of the most popular clustering algorithms. It partitions the data into K clusters, where each data point belongs to the cluster with the nearest mean. The algorithm iteratively updates the cluster centroids until convergence. K-means is widely used for customer segmentation, image compression, and anomaly detection, as it effectively identifies natural groupings within a dataset by minimizing the within-cluster variance.

Hierarchical Clustering: Hierarchical clustering builds a hierarchy of clusters using either an agglomerative (bottom-up) or divisive (top-down) approach. In agglomerative clustering, each data point starts as its own cluster, and pairs of clusters are merged iteratively based on their similarity. In divisive clustering, the entire dataset starts as one cluster, and it is recursively split into smaller clusters. This technique is useful for creating dendrograms that illustrate the hierarchical relationships between clusters, providing a visual and intuitive representation of the data's structure.

DBSCAN (Density-Based Spatial Clustering of Applications with Noise): DBSCAN is a density-based clustering algorithm that groups data points based on their density. It can identify clusters of arbitrary shape and is robust to noise and outliers. DBSCAN is particularly effective for spatial data and applications such as geographical mapping and image analysis, as it does not require specifying the number of clusters in advance and can automatically discover the optimal number of clusters based on the density of the data points.

Principal Component Analysis (PCA): PCA is a dimensionality reduction technique that transforms high-dimensional data into a lower-dimensional space while retaining as much variability as possible. It identifies the principal components (directions of maximum variance) in the data and projects the data onto these components. PCA is used for data visualization, noise reduction, and feature extraction. By reducing the number of dimensions, PCA helps simplify data and highlight its underlying structure.

t-Distributed Stochastic Neighbor Embedding (t-SNE): t-SNE is a non-linear dimensionality reduction technique that is particularly effective for visualizing high-dimensional data. It maps data points to a lower-dimensional space in a way that preserves the local structure of the data, making it useful for exploring clusters and patterns in complex datasets. t-SNE is widely used for visualizing data from domains such as genomics, image recognition, and natural language processing, where the relationships between data points are complex and non-linear.

Reinforcement Learning

Reinforcement learning involves an agent learning to make decisions by interacting with an environment. The agent receives rewards or penalties based on its actions, aiming to maximize cumulative rewards over time. This type of learning has been successfully applied in various fields, including robotics, game playing (e.g., AlphaGo), and autonomous vehicles. Reinforcement learning models are designed to learn optimal policies through trial and error, continuously improving their performance based on feedback from the environment.

Q-Learning: Q-learning is a model-free reinforcement learning algorithm that learns the value of actions in a given state. The agent updates its Q-values based on the rewards received and the estimated future rewards, eventually converging to an optimal policy. Q-learning is used in applications such as game playing and robotics. It is particularly effective in environments where the state and action spaces are discrete.

Deep Q-Networks (DQN): DQN is an extension of Q-learning that uses deep neural networks to approximate the Q-values. This allows the agent to handle high-dimensional state spaces and learn more complex policies. DQN has been used successfully in playing Atari games and other complex tasks. The combination of reinforcement learning and deep learning enables the agent to learn from raw sensory inputs, making it suitable for tasks that require high-level perception and decision-making.

Policy Gradient Methods: Policy gradient methods directly optimize the policy (the agent's decision-making strategy) by adjusting the policy parameters in the direction that increases the expected cumulative reward. These methods are used in applications such as robotic control and strategy optimization. Policy gradient methods are particularly effective for continuous action spaces, where the policy needs to be represented as a probability distribution over actions.

Building and Training Machine Learning Models

Building and training machine learning models is an iterative process. It involves selecting suitable algorithms, tuning hyperparameters, and evaluating model performance using metrics like accuracy, precision, recall, F1-score, and the area under the ROC curve (AUC-ROC). Model evaluation and validation are crucial to ensure the model generalizes well to new data. Techniques such as cross-validation, train-test splits, and bootstrapping help assess model performance and prevent overfitting.

Hyperparameter Tuning: Hyperparameter tuning involves adjusting the parameters that control the learning process (e.g., learning rate, number of trees in a random forest, or the number of layers in a neural network) to optimize model performance. Techniques like grid search, random search, and Bayesian optimization are commonly used for hyperparameter tuning. Proper tuning of hyperparameters can significantly improve model performance and stability.

Model Evaluation: Evaluating the performance of machine learning models is essential for selecting the best model and ensuring its reliability. Metrics like accuracy, precision, recall, F1-score, and AUC-ROC provide different perspectives on model performance, helping data scientists choose the most appropriate metric based on the problem and data characteristics. Model evaluation involves using holdout datasets or cross-validation techniques to assess how well the model performs on unseen data.

Cross-Validation: Cross-validation is a technique used to assess the generalizability of a model by partitioning the data into multiple training and validation sets. In K-fold cross-validation, the data is divided into K subsets (or folds). The model is trained on K-1 folds and validated on the remaining fold. This process is repeated K times, with each fold serving as the validation set once. The results are averaged to provide a robust estimate of model performance. Cross-validation helps prevent overfitting and ensures that the model performs well on unseen data.

Train-Test Split: Another common method for model evaluation is the train-test split, where the data is divided into two sets: a training set and a test set. The model is trained on the training set and evaluated on the test set. This method provides a straightforward way to assess model performance, though it may not be as robust as cross-validation. The train-test split is useful for providing a quick assessment of model performance and is often used as an initial step in model evaluation. It helps ensure that the model can generalize to new data by testing its performance on a separate subset that it has not seen during training.

Bootstrapping: Bootstrapping is a resampling technique that involves repeatedly sampling from the data with replacement to create multiple training sets. Each sample is used to train the model, and the performance is averaged across all samples. Bootstrapping provides an estimate of model performance and variability, making it useful for assessing model reliability. This technique helps in understanding the distribution of model performance metrics and can be particularly useful when the original dataset is small.

Advanced Machine Learning Techniques

Ensemble Methods: Ensemble methods combine multiple models to improve performance and robustness. Techniques like bagging, boosting, and stacking are commonly used to create ensemble models.

Bagging (Bootstrap Aggregating): Bagging involves training multiple models on different subsets of the data (created by bootstrapping) and averaging their predictions. Random forests are a popular example of a bagging technique. Bagging helps reduce variance and improve the stability of the model by averaging out the errors of individual models.

Boosting: Boosting is an iterative technique that trains multiple weak models sequentially, with each model correcting the errors of its predecessor. Gradient boosting and AdaBoost are well-known boosting algorithms. Boosting focuses on minimizing bias by combining weak learners to create a strong predictive model.

Stacking: Stacking involves training multiple base models and a meta-model that combines their predictions. The meta-model learns to weigh the contributions of each base model to produce a final prediction. Stacking can leverage the strengths of different algorithms to improve overall model performance.

Deep Learning: Deep learning techniques, such as convolutional neural networks (CNNs) and recurrent neural networks (RNNs), have revolutionized fields like image and speech recognition.

Convolutional Neural Networks (CNNs): CNNs are specialized neural networks designed for processing structured grid data, such as images. They use convolutional layers to automatically learn spatial hierarchies of features from the input data. CNNs are widely used in computer vision tasks, including image classification, object detection, and image segmentation. The hierarchical feature learning capability of CNNs makes them particularly powerful for visual data.

Recurrent Neural Networks (RNNs): RNNs are designed for sequential data, such as time series or text. They maintain a hidden state that captures information from previous time steps, allowing them to model temporal dependencies. RNNs and their variants, such as Long Short-Term Memory (LSTM) networks and Gated Recurrent Units

(GRUs), are used in natural language processing tasks like language modeling, machine translation, and sentiment analysis. The ability to capture temporal patterns makes RNNs suitable for dynamic data.

Practical Considerations

Feature Engineering: Creating and selecting the right features is critical for the success of machine learning models. Feature engineering involves transforming raw data into meaningful features that capture the underlying patterns in the data. Techniques like scaling, normalization, and encoding categorical variables are commonly used in feature engineering. Effective feature engineering can significantly enhance model performance by providing the model with informative and relevant input.

Model Interpretability: Ensuring that models are interpretable and transparent is important for building trust and making informed decisions. Techniques like feature importance, SHAP (SHapley Additive exPlanations), and LIME (Local Interpretable Model-agnostic Explanations) help explain model predictions and provide insights into how the model makes decisions. Model interpretability is crucial in applications where understanding the rationale behind predictions is essential, such as healthcare and finance.

Scalability: As data volumes grow, scalability becomes a critical consideration. Distributed computing frameworks like Apache Spark and Hadoop enable the processing of large datasets across multiple nodes, ensuring efficient and scalable machine learning workflows.

Scalability ensures that models can handle increasing data sizes and complexity without compromising performance.

Ethical Considerations: Ethical considerations, such as fairness, accountability, and transparency, are essential in machine learning. Data scientists must ensure that models do not perpetuate biases and are used responsibly. Developing and adhering to ethical guidelines and standards is crucial for maintaining public trust and ensuring the responsible use of machine learning. Ethical practices involve assessing potential biases in data and models, ensuring diverse representation, and documenting decision-making processes.

Real-World Applications

Healthcare: Machine learning models are used in healthcare for disease diagnosis, personalized treatment recommendations, and predictive analytics. For example, deep learning models can analyze medical images to detect tumors, while predictive models can forecast patient outcomes based on historical data. Machine learning aids in identifying disease patterns, optimizing treatment plans, and improving patient outcomes.

Finance: In finance, machine learning models are used for credit scoring, fraud detection, algorithmic trading, and risk management. For instance, classification models can identify fraudulent transactions, while regression models can predict stock prices. Machine learning enhances the ability to detect financial anomalies, assess credit risk accurately, and optimize investment strategies.

Retail: In retail, machine learning models are used for customer segmentation, demand forecasting, and recommendation systems. Clustering algorithms can segment customers based on purchasing behavior, while collaborative filtering techniques can recommend products to customers based on their preferences. Machine learning helps retailers personalize marketing efforts, optimize inventory management, and enhance customer experiences.

Manufacturing: Machine learning models are used in manufacturing for predictive maintenance, quality control, and process optimization. Predictive models can forecast equipment failures, while anomaly detection algorithms can identify defects in products. Machine learning improves operational efficiency, reduces downtime, and ensures product quality in manufacturing processes.

Transportation: In transportation, machine learning models are used for route optimization, traffic prediction, and autonomous driving. Reinforcement learning algorithms can optimize traffic light timings, while deep learning models can enable self-driving cars to navigate safely. Machine learning contributes to efficient logistics, reduced traffic congestion, and the development of autonomous vehicle technologies.

Key Points to Remember

Categories of Machine Learning: Machine learning models fall into three primary categories: supervised, unsupervised, and reinforcement learning. Each category includes various algorithms suited for different problems and data types. Understanding these categories helps data scientists select the appropriate algorithms for specific tasks.

Building and Training Models: Building and training machine learning models involves selecting algorithms, tuning hyperparameters, and evaluating performance using metrics like accuracy, precision, recall, F1-score, and AUC-ROC. Proper training and evaluation ensure that models are reliable and generalizable.

Advanced Techniques: Advanced techniques like ensemble methods and deep learning have significantly improved the performance and robustness of machine learning models. These techniques are used in various applications, from image recognition to natural language processing, leveraging multiple models to achieve better accuracy and reliability.

Practical Considerations: Feature engineering, model interpretability, scalability, and ethical considerations are crucial for the success and responsible use of machine learning models. Addressing these aspects ensures that models are effective, transparent, and fair.

Real-World Applications: Machine learning models have transformative applications across industries such as healthcare, finance, retail, manufacturing, and transportation. These applications demonstrate the value of machine learning in solving real-world problems and driving innovation.

By mastering machine learning techniques and understanding their practical applications, data scientists can build powerful models that deliver valuable insights and drive meaningful impact. Machine learning is a cornerstone of modern data science, enabling data scientists to harness the power of data to make predictions, optimize processes, and solve complex problems.

CHAPTER 8

REAL-WORLD APPLICATIONS

Data science has a transformative impact across various industries. In finance, it is used for fraud detection, risk management, and algorithmic trading. Machine learning models can analyze transaction patterns to detect fraudulent activities, predict credit risk, and optimize trading strategies. Predictive analytics and sentiment analysis help financial institutions make informed decisions and enhance customer experiences.

Financial Services

Fraud Detection: Financial institutions use machine learning models to detect fraudulent transactions in real-time. By analyzing transaction patterns and identifying anomalies, these models can flag suspicious activities and prevent financial losses. Techniques like logistic regression, decision trees, and neural networks are commonly used for fraud detection. These models continuously learn from new data, improving their ability to identify fraudulent activities.

Credit Scoring: Predictive models are used to assess the creditworthiness of individuals and businesses. By analyzing historical data and various financial indicators, these models can predict the likelihood of default, helping lenders make informed decisions. Techniques like logistic regression and random forests are commonly used for credit scoring. These models consider factors such as credit history, income, and employment status to assess credit risk accurately.

Algorithmic Trading: Machine learning models are used in algorithmic trading to develop trading strategies and optimize portfolio management. By analyzing market data and identifying patterns, these models can make buy and sell decisions at high speed, maximizing returns and minimizing risks. Techniques like reinforcement learning and deep learning are commonly used in algorithmic trading. These models adapt to changing market conditions, enabling more effective trading strategies.

Healthcare

Disease Diagnosis: Machine learning models are used to diagnose diseases and medical conditions by analyzing patient data, including medical records, imaging data, and genetic information. For example, deep learning models can analyze MRI scans to detect tumors, while classification models can predict the likelihood of diseases based on patient symptoms and history. Machine learning aids in early diagnosis, improving treatment outcomes and patient survival rates.

Personalized Medicine: Predictive models are used to develop personalized treatment plans based on individual patient characteristics and genetic profiles. By analyzing data from clinical trials and patient records, these models can recommend the most effective treatments for each patient. Techniques like clustering and regression are commonly used in personalized medicine. Personalized treatment plans enhance the effectiveness of therapies and reduce adverse effects.

Operational Efficiency: Data analytics is used to optimize hospital operations and resource allocation. Predictive models can forecast patient admissions and discharges, helping hospitals manage staffing and bed availability. Techniques like time series analysis and simulation modeling are commonly used for operational efficiency. Optimizing hospital operations ensures better patient care and efficient use of resources.

Retail

Customer Segmentation:

Retailers use clustering algorithms to segment customers based on purchasing behavior, demographics, and preferences. By understanding different customer segments, retailers can design targeted marketing campaigns and personalized promotions, improving customer engagement and retention. Techniques like K-means clustering and hierarchical clustering help identify distinct customer groups, enabling more effective marketing strategies. Customer segmentation allows retailers to tailor their offerings to specific customer needs, enhancing customer satisfaction and loyalty.

Demand Forecasting: Predictive models are used to forecast product demand, helping retailers manage inventory and supply chain operations. By analyzing historical sales data and external factors like seasonality and market trends, these models can predict future demand and optimize stock levels. Techniques like time series analysis, ARIMA models, and machine learning algorithms like random forests and neural networks are used for demand forecasting. Accurate demand forecasting ensures that retailers maintain optimal inventory levels, reducing stockouts and overstock situations.

Recommendation Systems: Retailers use recommendation systems to suggest products to customers based on their browsing and purchasing history. Techniques like collaborative filtering, content-based filtering, and matrix factorization are commonly used to develop recommendation systems that enhance the customer shopping experience and increase sales. By leveraging customer data, recommendation systems can provide personalized product suggestions, leading to higher conversion rates and increased customer satisfaction.

Manufacturing

Predictive Maintenance: By analyzing sensor data and historical maintenance records, machine learning models can identify patterns that indicate potential failures, thereby reducing downtime and maintenance costs. Techniques such as time series analysis, anomaly detection, and survival analysis are commonly used. Predictive maintenance not only enhances equipment reliability but also extends the lifespan of machinery, leading to significant cost savings and operational efficiency.

Quality Control: Data science is used to ensure product quality and consistency in manufacturing. Machine learning models can analyze production data to detect defects and deviations from quality standards. Techniques such as control charts, anomaly detection, and machine vision are employed to monitor production processes in real-time. By identifying issues early, manufacturers can take corrective actions promptly, reducing waste and improving product quality.

Supply Chain Optimization: Data science helps optimize supply chain operations by analyzing data on inventory levels, demand forecasts, and supplier performance. Predictive models can forecast demand, optimize inventory levels, and identify the best suppliers, leading to cost reductions and improved supply chain efficiency. Techniques such as linear programming, simulation modeling, and network analysis are used for supply chain optimization.

Energy Sector

Energy Consumption Optimization: Data science is used to analyze energy consumption patterns and identify opportunities for optimization. By analyzing data from smart meters and sensors, machine learning models can provide insights into energy usage and recommend ways to reduce consumption. Techniques such as time series analysis, clustering, and regression are commonly used. Optimizing energy consumption helps reduce costs and environmental impact.

Renewable Energy Management: Data science plays a crucial role in managing renewable energy sources such as wind and solar power. Predictive models can forecast energy production based on weather conditions and optimize the integration of renewable energy into the grid. Techniques such as regression, time series forecasting, and machine learning are used to manage renewable energy sources effectively. Effective management of renewable energy sources ensures a stable and sustainable energy supply.

Predictive Maintenance for Energy Infrastructure: Similar to manufacturing, predictive maintenance is used to ensure the reliability of energy infrastructure. By analyzing data from sensors and maintenance records, machine learning models can predict equipment failures and schedule maintenance proactively. This approach reduces downtime and maintenance costs, ensuring the efficient operation of energy infrastructure.

Transportation

Route Optimization: Data science is used to optimize routes for transportation and logistics. By analyzing traffic data, weather conditions, and delivery schedules, machine learning models can identify the most efficient routes, reducing travel time and fuel consumption. Techniques such as shortest path algorithms, simulation modeling, and optimization algorithms are commonly used. Optimizing routes ensures timely deliveries and reduces operational costs.

Traffic Prediction: Predictive models are used to forecast traffic conditions and congestion. By analyzing historical traffic data and real-time sensor data, machine learning models can predict traffic patterns and provide insights for traffic management and planning. Techniques such as time series analysis, regression, and machine learning are used for traffic prediction. Accurate traffic prediction helps in reducing congestion and improving traffic flow.

Autonomous Vehicles: Data science and machine learning are integral to the development of autonomous vehicles. Machine learning models are used to process data from sensors and cameras, enabling vehicles to navigate and make decisions in real-time. Techniques such as deep learning, reinforcement learning, and computer vision are used to develop autonomous driving systems. Autonomous vehicles have the potential to revolutionize transportation by improving safety and efficiency.

Public Sector

- Policy Analysis: Data science is used to analyze the impact of public policies and inform decision-making. Predictive models can forecast the outcomes of policy changes, helping policymakers make informed decisions. Techniques such as regression analysis, simulation modeling, and machine learning are commonly used in policy analysis. Data-driven policy analysis helps in formulating effective and sustainable public policies.

- Public Health Monitoring: Data science plays a crucial role in monitoring public health and managing epidemics. By analyzing data on disease outbreaks, vaccination rates, and population health, machine learning models can predict the spread of diseases and inform public health interventions. Techniques such as time series analysis, spatial analysis, and machine learning are used for public health monitoring. Effective public health monitoring ensures timely and targeted interventions.

- Urban Planning: Data science helps urban planners design smarter and more sustainable cities. By analyzing data on population growth, transportation, and infrastructure, predictive models can provide insights into urban development and resource allocation. Techniques such as geographic information systems (GIS), simulation modeling, and network analysis are used in urban planning. Data-driven urban planning helps in creating efficient and livable urban environments.

Education

Personalized Learning: Data science is used to develop personalized learning experiences for students. By analyzing data on student performance, learning styles, and engagement, machine learning models can recommend personalized learning paths and resources. Techniques such as clustering, collaborative filtering, and regression are commonly used in personalized learning. Personalized learning enhances student engagement and academic performance.

Student Performance Prediction: Predictive models are used to forecast student performance and identify at-risk students. By analyzing data on academic performance, attendance, and socio-economic factors, machine learning models can predict student outcomes and inform interventions. Techniques such as logistic regression, decision trees, and neural networks are used for student performance prediction. Early identification of at-risk students helps in providing timely support and improving educational outcomes.

Administrative Efficiency: Data science helps educational institutions optimize administrative processes such as admissions, scheduling, and resource allocation. Predictive models can forecast enrollment trends, optimize class schedules, and allocate resources effectively. Techniques such as time series analysis, simulation modeling, and optimization algorithms are used to improve administrative efficiency. Efficient administration ensures better management of educational resources and enhances institutional performance.

Entertainment

Content Recommendation: Streaming platforms and media companies use machine learning models to recommend content to users based on their viewing history and preferences. Techniques such as collaborative filtering, content-based filtering, and matrix factorization are commonly used to develop recommendation systems. Personalized content recommendations enhance user experience and engagement.

Audience Analysis: Data science is used to analyze audience demographics and preferences, guiding content creation and marketing strategies. By analyzing data on viewer behavior, media companies can identify trends and develop targeted marketing campaigns. Techniques such as clustering, regression, and sentiment analysis are used for audience analysis. Understanding audience preferences helps in creating content that resonates with viewers.

Production Optimization: Data science helps optimize production processes in the entertainment industry. By analyzing data on production schedules, costs, and resource utilization, machine learning models can identify inefficiencies and recommend improvements. Techniques such as simulation modeling, optimization algorithms, and machine learning are used to optimize production processes. Efficient production management ensures timely and cost-effective content creation.

Key Points to Remember

Impact Across Industries: Data science has a transformative impact across various industries, including finance, healthcare, retail, manufacturing, energy, transportation, public sector, education, and entertainment. Understanding the broad applications of data science helps in leveraging its potential for diverse business challenges.

Techniques and Algorithms: Various machine learning techniques and algorithms, such as clustering, regression, decision trees, neural networks, and deep learning, are used to analyze data and derive insights. Mastery of these techniques enables data scientists to solve complex problems effectively.

Real-World Applications: Data science applications range from fraud detection and personalized medicine to route optimization and content recommendation. These applications demonstrate the value of data-driven insights in solving real-world problems. Applying data science to practical scenarios drives innovation and operational efficiency.

Challenges and Solutions: Data scientists must address challenges such as data privacy, scalability, and ethical considerations to ensure the responsible and effective use of data science. Overcoming these challenges requires continuous learning, innovation, and adherence to best practices.

Future Directions: Innovations in machine learning, AI, and data analytics are driving the future of data science, enabling new applications and improving the accuracy and efficiency of data-driven insights. Staying updated with these advancements is crucial for leveraging cutting-edge technologies.

By understanding the real-world applications and impact of data science, data scientists can leverage their skills to drive innovation and solve complex problems across various domains. The ability to analyze data and derive actionable insights is a powerful tool for creating value and achieving strategic goals.

CHAPTER 9

CHALLENGES AND SOLUTIONS

Data scientists frequently encounter numerous challenges in their work. Common obstacles include data privacy concerns, integration of disparate data sources, and scalability issues. Ensuring data privacy and security is paramount, especially when handling sensitive information. Techniques like differential privacy, federated learning, and homomorphic encryption help protect individual privacy while enabling data analysis.

Data Privacy and Security

Differential Privacy: Differential privacy is a technique that adds noise to data to ensure that individual data points cannot be identified. It allows data scientists to analyze data and derive insights without compromising privacy. Differential privacy is widely used in scenarios where data anonymization is crucial, such as healthcare and finance.

By adding controlled noise, differential privacy maintains the overall utility of the data while protecting individual privacy.

Federated Learning: Federated learning is a technique that allows machine learning models to be trained across multiple decentralized devices or servers while keeping the data localized. This approach enhances data privacy and security by ensuring that sensitive data remains on local devices, reducing the risk of data breaches. Federated learning is particularly useful in scenarios where data cannot be centralized due to privacy regulations, such as in healthcare or finance. By enabling collaborative model training without data sharing, federated learning facilitates the development of robust models while maintaining data confidentiality.

Homomorphic Encryption: Homomorphic encryption allows computations to be performed on encrypted data without decrypting it. This technique ensures data privacy and security during data analysis and machine learning tasks. Homomorphic encryption is used in scenarios where data confidentiality is critical, such as cloud computing and secure data sharing. It allows for secure processing of sensitive information, ensuring that data remains protected throughout its lifecycle.

Integration of Disparate Data Sources

Integrating data from various sources can be challenging due to differences in formats, structures, and semantics. Data integration platforms and ETL (Extract, Transform, Load) processes harmonize data from multiple sources, enabling comprehensive data analysis and insights.

ETL Processes: ETL processes involve extracting data from various sources, transforming it into a consistent format, and loading it into a data warehouse or data lake. These processes ensure data consistency and enable efficient data integration and analysis. ETL tools like Apache NiFi, Talend, and Informatica are widely used to streamline data integration workflows.

Data Warehousing: Data warehousing involves consolidating data from multiple sources into a central repository. Data warehouses provide a unified view of data and support complex queries and analytics. Techniques like star schema and snowflake schema are used to organize data in data warehouses. Data warehouses enable organizations to perform advanced analytics and business intelligence, driving data-driven decision-making.

Data Lakes: Data lakes are scalable storage repositories that store raw data in its native format. Data lakes support various data types, including structured, semi-structured, and unstructured data. They enable flexible data ingestion and analysis, making them suitable for big data and analytics. Tools like Apache Hadoop and Amazon S3 are commonly used to build and manage data lakes, providing a cost-effective solution for storing vast amounts of data.

Scalability Issues

Scalability issues arise when dealing with large data volumes. Cloud-based data platforms, distributed computing, and big data technologies like Hadoop and Spark address these challenges, enabling efficient data processing and analysis.

Cloud Computing: Cloud platforms such as AWS, Google Cloud, and Microsoft Azure provide scalable infrastructure and services for data storage, processing, and analysis. Cloud computing enables organizations to handle large datasets and scale their data science workflows efficiently. Cloud services offer flexibility, allowing organizations to adjust resources based on demand, ensuring cost-effective scalability.

Distributed Computing: Distributed computing frameworks like Hadoop and Spark enable parallel processing of large datasets across multiple nodes. These frameworks provide the infrastructure needed to process and analyze big data efficiently. Hadoop's HDFS (Hadoop Distributed File System) allows for distributed storage, while Spark's in-memory processing capabilities significantly speed up data processing tasks.

Big Data Technologies: Big data technologies, such as Hadoop's HDFS and Apache Spark, provide the infrastructure needed to store and process large volumes of data efficiently. HDFS allows for distributed storage of massive datasets across multiple nodes, while Spark enables in-memory data processing, significantly speeding up data analysis tasks. These technologies are essential for handling big data and scaling data science workflows.

Innovation and Collaboration

Innovation and collaboration are vital to overcoming these challenges. Data scientists must continuously explore new techniques, stay updated with advancements, and work closely with domain experts and stakeholders to develop effective solutions. Open-source communities and professional networks provide valuable resources for learning, collaboration, and problem-solving.

Open-Source Communities: Open-source communities, such as GitHub, offer a wealth of resources, including libraries, frameworks, and code repositories. Engaging with these communities allows data scientists to share knowledge, collaborate on projects, and stay updated with the latest advancements in data science. Contributing to open-source projects also provides opportunities for professional growth and skill development.

Professional Networks: Professional networks, such as LinkedIn and industry-specific forums, provide opportunities for networking, learning, and career development. Participating in conferences, webinars, and workshops helps data scientists stay current with industry trends and best practices. Networking with peers and mentors can lead to new collaborations and career opportunities.

Ensuring Interpretability and Transparency

Ensuring the interpretability and transparency of machine learning models is crucial for building trust with stakeholders and making informed decisions. Complex models, such as deep learning networks, can be difficult to interpret, raising concerns about their decision-making processes.

Model Interpretability: Techniques like SHAP (SHapley Additive exPlanations) and LIME (Local Interpretable Model-agnostic Explanations) help improve model interpretability by explaining the contributions of individual features to the model's predictions. These techniques provide insights into how models make decisions, enabling data scientists to validate and refine their models. Model interpretability is essential for gaining stakeholder trust and ensuring responsible AI deployment.

Transparency in Decision-Making: Transparent decision-making involves documenting the methods, assumptions, and rationale behind model development and deployment. This transparency ensures that stakeholders understand and trust the analysis, facilitating data-driven decision-making. Clear documentation and communication of model development processes enhance accountability and ethical compliance.

Ethical Considerations

Ethical considerations are crucial in data science. Data scientists must ensure that their analyses and models are fair, unbiased, and do not perpetuate discrimination. This involves carefully selecting features, evaluating potential biases, and implementing fairness-aware algorithms.

Bias Detection and Mitigation: Bias in data and models can lead to unfair outcomes and discrimination. Techniques such as re-sampling, adjusting weights, and employing fairness-aware algorithms help detect and mitigate bias, ensuring that models are fair and equitable. Regular audits and evaluations of models are necessary to identify and address potential biases.

Ethical Guidelines and Standards: Developing and adhering to ethical guidelines and standards is essential for maintaining public trust and ensuring the responsible use of data science. Organizations should establish ethical frameworks and best practices to guide data scientists in their work. Ethical guidelines help ensure that data science practices align with societal values and legal requirements.

Continuous Learning and Professional Development

Data scientists must manage the challenge of keeping their skills and knowledge up to date in a rapidly evolving field. Continuous learning and professional development are essential for staying current with new technologies, methodologies, and best practices.

Workshops and Conferences: Attending workshops, conferences, and webinars provides opportunities for learning, networking, and staying updated with industry advancements. These events offer insights into the latest trends, tools, and techniques in data science. Conferences like the ACM SIGKDD Conference on Knowledge Discovery and Data Mining and the IEEE International Conference on Data Mining are valuable for professional development.

Online Courses and Certifications: Online learning platforms, such as Coursera, edX, and Udacity, offer a wide range of courses and certifications in data science. These courses provide flexible learning options and help data scientists acquire new skills and stay competitive in the job market. Certifications from recognized institutions enhance professional credibility and career prospects.

Engaging with the Community: Participating in online forums, professional networks, and open-source communities helps data scientists stay connected with peers, share knowledge, and collaborate on projects. Engaging with the data science community fosters continuous learning and professional growth. Platforms like

Kaggle and Data Science Central offer opportunities for collaboration and skill development.

Key Points to Remember

Data Privacy and Security: Ensuring data privacy and security is paramount, especially when handling sensitive information. Techniques like differential privacy, federated learning, and homomorphic encryption help protect individual privacy while enabling data analysis. Maintaining robust data security measures is essential for building trust and compliance with regulations.

Integration and Scalability: Integrating data from various sources and scaling data science workflows are critical challenges. Cloud computing, distributed computing, and big data technologies like Hadoop and Spark address these challenges, enabling efficient data processing and analysis. Effective data integration and scalable infrastructure support advanced analytics and business intelligence.

Interpretability and Transparency: Ensuring the interpretability and transparency of machine learning models is crucial for building trust and making informed decisions. Techniques like SHAP and LIME improve model interpretability, while transparent decision-making fosters trust and accountability. Clear communication of model assumptions and methodologies enhances stakeholder confidence.

Ethical Considerations: Ethical considerations, such as fairness, accountability, and transparency, are essential in data science. Bias detection, fairness-aware algorithms, and ethical guidelines help ensure responsible and equitable use of data science. Ethical practices align data science initiatives with societal values and legal standards.

Continuous Learning: The field of data science is dynamic and rapidly evolving. Continuous learning and professional development are essential for staying current with new technologies, methodologies, and best practices. Workshops, conferences, online courses, and community engagement are valuable resources for professional growth. Lifelong learning ensures that data scientists remain adaptable and innovative.

By understanding and addressing these challenges, data scientists can enhance the quality, reliability, and ethical standards of their work. Overcoming these obstacles requires continuous learning, innovation, and collaboration, enabling data scientists to drive meaningful impact and create value across various domains. Maintaining high ethical standards ensures that data science practices contribute positively to society, building trust and fostering sustainable growth.

Data science is a powerful tool that enables organizations to derive valuable insights from data, solve complex problems, and drive innovation. By mastering various machine learning techniques, addressing challenges related to data privacy, integration, and scalability, and upholding ethical standards, data scientists can create meaningful impact across diverse industries. Continuous learning, collaboration, and innovation are essential for staying at the forefront of the field and leveraging emerging technologies to unlock new opportunities.

As data science continues to evolve, its applications and impact will expand, transforming industries and improving lives. By embracing the potential of data science and committing to ethical and responsible practices, data scientists can contribute to a better and more informed world, where data-driven insights lead to smarter decisions, sustainable growth, and positive societal change.

CHAPTER 10

THE FUTURE OF DATA SCIENCE

The future of data science is promising, propelled by advancements in artificial intelligence (AI), quantum computing, and the Internet of Things (IoT). AI is expanding the boundaries of possibility, enabling machines to perform complex tasks traditionally done by humans. AI-powered applications, such as autonomous vehicles and personalized recommendations, are transforming industries and everyday life.

Artificial Intelligence (AI)

AI is revolutionizing data science by enabling machines to learn from data and make intelligent decisions. Advances in machine learning, deep learning, and natural language processing (NLP) are driving the development of AI-powered applications across various domains.

Machine Learning and Deep Learning: Machine learning and deep learning are at the forefront of AI research and development. Techniques such as neural networks, convolutional neural networks (CNNs), and recurrent neural networks (RNNs) are being used to build sophisticated AI models for tasks like image recognition, speech processing, and natural language understanding. As these models become more advanced, they can handle increasingly complex tasks, from diagnosing diseases to predicting market trends.

Natural Language Processing (NLP: NLP is a rapidly advancing field that focuses on the interaction between computers and human language. Techniques such as transformer models (e.g., BERT, GPT) are enabling machines to understand and generate human language with remarkable accuracy, leading to advancements in chatbots, virtual assistants, and language translation. NLP is also being used to analyze large volumes of text data, extracting insights and automating tasks like sentiment analysis and content moderation.

Quantum Computing

Quantum computing promises to solve problems currently unsolvable by classical computers. By leveraging quantum mechanics, quantum computers can process vast amounts of data simultaneously, potentially revolutionizing fields like cryptography, optimization, and materials science. Quantum machine learning, an emerging field, merges quantum computing and machine learning to create new algorithms and techniques.

- Quantum Machine Learning: Quantum machine learning combines the principles of quantum computing and machine learning to develop algorithms that can process and analyze data more efficiently than classical methods. This emerging field holds the potential to revolutionize data science by enabling faster and more accurate data analysis. Quantum algorithms, such as quantum support vector machines and quantum neural networks, are being explored to solve complex problems in areas like drug discovery and financial modeling.

- Quantum Cryptography: Quantum cryptography leverages the principles of quantum mechanics to develop secure communication protocols that are theoretically immune to hacking. This technology has significant implications for data privacy and security, ensuring that sensitive information is protected from unauthorized access. Quantum key distribution (QKD) is one example of quantum cryptography, providing a secure method for exchanging encryption keys.

Internet of Things (IoT)

The IoT is generating unprecedented amounts of data, creating new opportunities for data science. IoT devices, ranging from smart home appliances to industrial sensors, provide real-time data streams that can be analyzed to optimize operations, enhance user experiences, and improve safety and efficiency.

- Real-Time Analytics: IoT devices generate continuous data streams that require real-time analysis to derive actionable insights. Edge computing and real-time analytics enable data processing closer to the source, reducing latency and enhancing decision-making capabilities. For example, in smart manufacturing, sensors on production lines can monitor equipment performance in real-time, predicting maintenance needs and preventing downtime.

- Smart Cities: IoT technologies are transforming urban environments into smart cities, where data from connected devices is used to optimize infrastructure, improve public services, and enhance the quality of life for residents. Data science plays a crucial role in analyzing and interpreting IoT data to drive smart city initiatives. Applications include intelligent traffic management systems, smart grids for efficient energy use, and real-time air quality monitoring to reduce pollution.

Interdisciplinary Collaboration

Interdisciplinary collaboration will be key to addressing complex challenges and driving innovation in data science. Data scientists will need to work closely with experts from various fields, including domain specialists, policymakers, and ethicists, to develop holistic and impactful solutions.

- Domain Expertise: Collaborating with domain experts ensures that data science solutions are grounded in a deep understanding of the specific context and challenges of the field. Whether it's healthcare, finance, or environmental science, domain expertise provides critical insights that guide data analysis and model development. For example, in healthcare, working with clinicians and medical researchers helps ensure that predictive models are clinically relevant and actionable.

- Policy and Regulation: Working with policymakers and regulatory bodies helps ensure that data science applications comply with legal and ethical standards. This collaboration is crucial for developing policies that protect data privacy, promote transparency, and ensure the responsible use of data science technologies. Engaging with regulators early in the development process can help identify potential legal and ethical issues and develop strategies to address them.

- Ethics and Philosophy: Engaging with ethicists and philosophers helps address the broader ethical implications of data science. This interdisciplinary approach ensures that data science practices align with societal values and ethical principles, promoting fairness, accountability, and transparency. Ethicists can provide guidance on issues such as consent, privacy, and the societal impact of AI technologies.

Emerging Technologies and Trends

Several emerging technologies and trends are shaping the future of data science, offering new opportunities and challenges.

- Blockchain Technology: Blockchain technology, known for its security and transparency, can enhance data integrity and trustworthiness in data science applications. By providing a decentralized and tamper-proof ledger, blockchain ensures the authenticity and security of data, making it valuable for applications such as supply chain management, healthcare, and finance. For example, in supply chain management, blockchain can provide a transparent and immutable record of product origins and movements, ensuring traceability and reducing fraud.

- 5G Networks: The proliferation of 5G networks will enable faster data transmission and improved connectivity, facilitating the real-time analysis of large and complex datasets. This advancement will enhance the capabilities of IoT devices and support the development of smart cities and autonomous systems. With higher data transfer speeds and lower latency, 5G networks will enable new applications in areas such as remote surgery, augmented reality, and connected vehicles.

- Explainable AI (XAI): Explainable AI focuses on making machine learning models more transparent and interpretable. Techniques such as SHAP and LIME help explain model predictions, enabling stakeholders to understand and trust AI decisions. XAI is essential for ensuring the ethical and responsible use of AI technologies, particularly in high-stakes domains like healthcare, finance, and criminal justice.

Personalized and Adaptive Systems

The future of data science holds exciting possibilities for personalized and adaptive learning systems, healthcare, and consumer experiences.

- Personalized Learning: Leveraging AI and data analytics, educational platforms can tailor learning experiences to individual needs and preferences, enhancing student engagement and outcomes. Personalized learning systems provide real-time feedback, identify areas for improvement, and adapt learning materials to suit the pace and style of each learner. AI-driven tutoring systems and adaptive learning platforms are transforming education by providing customized support and resources for students.

- Precision Medicine: In healthcare, the integration of data science and AI will advance precision medicine. By analyzing genetic information, medical histories, and lifestyle data, predictive models can provide personalized treatment plans and early detection of diseases. AI-powered diagnostic tools can assist healthcare professionals in making accurate and timely decisions, improving patient outcomes and reducing healthcare costs. Precision medicine aims to move from a one-size-fits-all approach to tailored treatments based on individual patient profiles.

- Enhanced Consumer Experiences: Data science will continue to drive innovation in personalized marketing, customer service, and product recommendations. By analyzing consumer behavior and preferences, businesses can deliver tailored experiences that meet individual needs and expectations, fostering customer loyalty and satisfaction. AI-driven recommendation engines, chatbots, and personalized advertising are examples of how data science enhances consumer experiences.

Environmental and Social Impact

Data science has the potential to address pressing environmental and social challenges, promoting sustainability and improving the quality of life.

Climate Change and Sustainability: Predictive analytics and machine learning models can help monitor and address climate change, optimize resource management, and promote sustainable practices. Data-driven models can predict weather patterns, track deforestation, and optimize energy consumption in smart grids, contributing to environmental conservation and sustainability. For example, predictive models can forecast the impact of climate change on agriculture, helping farmers adapt their practices and improve crop yields.

Social Good: Data science can be leveraged to address social issues such as poverty, healthcare access, and education. By analyzing data on social determinants, predictive models can identify vulnerable populations, inform policy decisions, and drive initiatives that improve social welfare and equity. Data-driven approaches can help design effective interventions, allocate resources efficiently, and measure the impact of social programs.

Key Points to Remember

AI and Machine Learning: Advances in AI and machine learning are driving the development of sophisticated models and applications that transform industries and everyday life. AI technologies enable machines to perform complex tasks, improve decision-making, and improve decision-making, and enhance user experiences. From healthcare diagnostics to autonomous vehicles, AI is making significant strides in various sectors, creating more efficient and intelligent systems.

Quantum Computing: Quantum computing holds the potential to revolutionize data science by enabling faster and more accurate data analysis, solving problems currently unsolvable by classical computers. Quantum algorithms, such as quantum machine learning and quantum cryptography, are paving the way for breakthroughs in fields like optimization, drug discovery, and secure communications.

IoT and Real-Time Analytics: The IoT is generating vast amounts of data, creating opportunities for real-time analytics and smart applications. Edge computing and 5G networks are enhancing the capabilities of IoT devices, enabling real-time data processing and decision-making in areas like smart cities, industrial automation, and healthcare monitoring.

Interdisciplinary Collaboration: Collaboration with domain experts, policymakers, and ethicists is essential for developing holistic and impactful data science solutions. Interdisciplinary approaches ensure that data science practices align with societal values and ethical principles, enhancing the relevance and acceptance of data-driven insights and applications.

Emerging Technologies: Technologies such as blockchain, 5G networks, and explainable AI are shaping the future of data science, offering new opportunities and challenges. These technologies enhance data integrity, connectivity, and transparency, supporting the development of more robust and trustworthy data science solutions.

Personalized Systems: Personalized and adaptive systems in education, healthcare, and consumer experiences are driving innovation and improving outcomes. Data science enables the creation of tailored experiences that meet individual needs and preferences, enhancing user satisfaction and engagement.

Environmental and Social Impact: Data science has the potential to address environmental and social challenges, promoting sustainability and improving the quality of life. Predictive analytics and machine learning models can optimize resource management, monitor climate change, and support social initiatives that improve welfare and equity.

By embracing continuous learning and staying ahead of trends, data scientists can lead the way in solving complex problems and creating a better future for all. The future of data science is bright, and the possibilities are limitless. As we continue this journey, let us strive to harness the power of data for the greater good and create a world where data-driven insights lead to better decisions, improved outcomes, and a brighter future for all.

The Importance of Soft Skills

While technical skills are crucial for data scientists, soft skills are equally important. Effective communication, problem-solving, and critical thinking skills enable data scientists to translate complex data insights into actionable business strategies. Collaboration and teamwork are essential for working effectively with cross-functional teams and stakeholders.

- Communication Skills: Data scientists must be able to communicate their findings clearly and effectively to non-technical stakeholders. This includes presenting data visualizations, writing reports, and explaining complex concepts in simple terms.

- Problem-Solving Skills: The ability to approach problems methodically and creatively is essential for data scientists. This involves identifying the root cause of issues, generating potential solutions, and evaluating the effectiveness of different approaches.

- Critical Thinking: Critical thinking skills enable data scientists to evaluate data objectively, question assumptions, and make informed decisions. This involves analyzing data from multiple perspectives and considering the broader context.

The Growing Demand for Data Scientists

The demand for data scientists is growing rapidly across various industries. As organizations increasingly rely on data to drive decision-making, the need for skilled data professionals continues to rise. This demand is creating numerous job opportunities and driving competitive salaries for data scientists.

- Industry Demand: Industries such as healthcare, finance, retail, and technology are leading the demand for data scientists. These sectors are leveraging data to enhance operational efficiency, improve customer experiences, and drive innovation.

- Career Opportunities: The growing demand for data scientists is creating diverse career opportunities, from entry-level positions to senior leadership roles. Data scientists can specialize in areas such as machine learning, big data analytics, or AI, or pursue roles in data strategy and governance.

- Competitive Salaries: The high demand for data scientists, coupled with the specialized skills required, is driving competitive salaries. Organizations are offering attractive compensation packages to attract and retain top talent.

The Future Landscape of Data Science Careers

As the field of data science evolves, so too will the career landscape. Emerging roles such as AI ethics officers, data privacy officers, and AI strategy consultants will become increasingly important. Data scientists will also need to adapt to new technologies and methodologies, such as quantum computing and edge AI.

- Emerging Roles: The rise of AI and data-driven decision-making is creating new roles focused on ethical considerations, data privacy, and strategic implementation. AI ethics officers will ensure that AI systems are developed and used responsibly, while data privacy officers will focus on protecting sensitive information.

- Adaptation to New Technologies: Data scientists must stay ahead of technological advancements and continuously update their skills. This includes learning about quantum computing, edge AI, and other emerging technologies that will shape the future of data science.

FINAL NOTES

Reflecting on the journey of data science, several key takeaways emerge. These insights can guide aspiring data scientists and professionals in the field as they navigate the complexities and opportunities ahead.

Embrace Continuous Learning: The field of data science is dynamic and ever-changing. Continuous learning is essential for staying current with new technologies, methodologies, and best practices. Engaging in lifelong learning through courses, workshops, and professional development is crucial.

Cultivate Soft Skills: Technical skills alone are not enough. Data scientists must also cultivate soft skills such as communication, problem-solving, and critical thinking. These skills enable effective collaboration and the translation of data insights into actionable strategies.

Stay Ethical and Responsible: Ethical considerations must be at the forefront of data science practices. Ensuring fairness, transparency, and accountability is essential for building trust and driving positive societal impact. Data scientists have a responsibility to use their skills for the greater good.

Leverage Interdisciplinary Collaboration: Collaboration with experts from various fields enhances the relevance and impact of data science solutions. Interdisciplinary approaches are essential for addressing complex challenges and developing innovative solutions.

Prepare for the Future: The future of data science holds tremendous potential, driven by advancements in AI, quantum computing, and the IoT. Data scientists must prepare for emerging roles and technologies, staying adaptable and ready to embrace new opportunities.

As we reflect on the transformative power of data science, it becomes clear that the field is not just about analyzing data but about making a meaningful impact on the world. Data scientists have the opportunity to drive innovation, solve complex problems, and create solutions that improve lives. By embracing curiosity, creativity, and ethical responsibility, data scientists can unlock the full potential of data and contribute to a brighter future.

The journey of a data scientist is one of continuous exploration and growth. It is a path filled with challenges, discoveries, and opportunities to make a positive difference. As we move forward, let us remain committed to the principles that guide us, leveraging the power of data to create a better world for all.

The future of data science is bright, and the possibilities are limitless. By staying curious, embracing challenges, and committing to ethical practices, data scientists can drive innovation and create solutions that make a positive difference in the world. Let us continue to explore, learn, and innovate, shaping the future of data science and unlocking the full potential of data for the betterment of society.

INDEX

APPENDICES

Appendix A: Glossary of Key Terms

Algorithm: A set of rules or steps used to solve a problem.

Artificial Intelligence (AI): The simulation of human intelligence processes by machines, especially computer systems.

Big Data: Extremely large data sets that may be analyzed computationally to reveal patterns, trends, and associations.

Clustering: A technique used to group similar data points together.

Data Science: A field that uses scientific methods, processes, algorithms, and systems to extract knowledge and insights from structured and unstructured data.

Deep Learning: A subset of machine learning involving neural networks with many layers.

Machine Learning: A method of data analysis that automates analytical model building.

*Predictive Analytics: The practice of extracting information from existing data sets to determine patterns and predict future outcomes and trends.

Appendix B: Recommended Resources

Books

"The Elements of Statistical Learning" by Trevor Hastie, Robert Tibshirani, and Jerome Friedman

"Pattern Recognition and Machine Learning" by Christopher Bishop

"Deep Learning" by Ian Goodfellow, Yoshua Bengio, and Aaron Courville

Online Courses

Coursera: Machine Learning by Andrew Ng

edX: Data Science MicroMasters Program by UC San Diego

Udacity: Data Scientist Nanodegree Program

Websites and Blogs

Towards Data Science

KDnuggets

Data Science Central

Appendix C: Data Science Tools and Libraries

Python: Pandas, NumPy, Scikit-learn, TensorFlow, Keras

R: ggplot2, dplyr, caret, randomForest

Data Visualization: Tableau, Power BI, Matplotlib, Seaborn

Big Data: Apache Hadoop, Apache Spark

Databases: SQL, MongoDB, PostgreSQL

Appendix D: Ethical Guidelines in Data Science

Fairness: Ensure algorithms do not perpetuate bias or discrimination.

Transparency: Maintain transparency in data collection, model development, and decision-making processes.

Privacy: Protect individual privacy and comply with data protection regulations.

Accountability: Ensure accountability for the outcomes of data science projects.

Appendix E: Case Studies

Healthcare

Predictive models for patient readmission

Early detection of diseases using machine learning

Retail

Customer segmentation and personalized marketing strategies

Inventory management and demand forecasting

Finance

Fraud detection in financial transactions

Credit risk assessment models

Manufacturing

Predictive maintenance for machinery

Quality control and optimization

Energy

Renewable energy management

Predictive maintenance for energy infrastructure

Transportation

Route optimization for logistics

Traffic prediction and management

Agriculture

Precision Farming: Utilizing data analytics to monitor soil conditions, optimize irrigation, and manage crop health, resulting in higher yields and sustainable farming practices.

Supply Chain Optimization: Applying predictive analytics to streamline the agricultural supply chain, reducing waste and ensuring timely delivery of produce.

Education

Personalized Learning: Implementing adaptive learning systems that tailor educational content to individual student needs, improving learning outcomes.

Student Performance Analysis: Using predictive models to identify at-risk students and develop intervention strategies to support their success.

Public Sector

Policy Analysis: Analyzing data to inform public policy decisions, improve resource allocation, and enhance the effectiveness of government programs.

Public Health Monitoring: Leveraging data science to track and manage public health issues, including disease outbreaks and vaccination efforts.